A Common Workbook

JOHN H. RILEY, JR.

Prentice Hall
Englewood Cliffs, New Jersey 07632

Library of Congress Cataloging-in-Publication Data

Riley, John H.
    A common Lisp workbook / John H. Riley, Jr.
      p. cm.
      ISBN 0-13-155797-1
      1. Common LISP (Computer program language) I. Title.
    QA76.73.C62R55   1991
    005.13'3—dc20   91-33680
                                                                                    CIP

Acquisition Editor: Marcia Horton
Production Editors: Fred Dahl and Rose Kernan
Copy Editor: Rose Kernan
Designer: Fred Dahl
Cover Designer: Wanda Lubelska
Cover Illustrator: Don Martinetti
Prepress Buyer: Linda Behrens
Manufacturing Buyer: David Dickey
Supplements Editor: Alice Dworkin

 © 1992 by Prentice-Hall, Inc.
A Simon & Schuster Company
Englewood Cliffs, New Jersey 07632

All rights reserved. No part of this book may be
reproduced in any form or by any means
without permission in writing from the publisher.

Printed in the United States of America
10 9 8 7 6 5 4 3 2 1

ISBN 0-13-155797-1

Prentice-Hall International (UK) Limited, *London*
Prentice-Hall of Australia Pty. Limited, *Sydney*
Prentice-Hall Canada Inc., *Toronto*
Prentice-Hall Hispanoamericana, S.A., *Mexico*
Prentice-Hall of India Private Limited, *New Delhi*
Prentice-Hall of Japan, Inc., *Tokyo*
Simon & Schuster Asia Pte. Ltd., *Singapore*
Editora Prentice-Hall do Brasil, Ltda., *Rio de Janeiro*

CONTENTS

Preface, *viii*

Preliminaries, *ix*
    Running LISP and operating system details. Lisp conventions.

LESSON 1

Using LISP, *1*
    Basic variable, expression and arithmetic manipulation.

+	quote
−	'
*	setf
	setq

LESSON 2

List Manipulation (1), *10*
    Construction and manipulation of lists.

car	cons
cdr	caar
first	cadr
rest	cdar
nil ( )	cddr

LESSON 3

Defining Functions, *22*
    Defining functions, particularly recursive functions.

defun	listp
t	cond
numberp	1+
symbolp	trace
null	untrace

LESSON 4

Controlling Execution Flow (1), *36*
    Comparisons, predicates and control functions. Output.

eql	or
format (using ~a)	if
atom	when
not	unless
and	zerop

LESSON 5
List Manipulation (2), *51*
    Useful functions for working with lists.

append	ninth
list	tenth
second	length
third	reverse
fourth	max
fifth	min
sixth	rplaca
seventh	rplacd
eighth	

LESSON 6
The Common LISP Programming Environment, *65*
    Obtaining information about the environment. System functions. Debugging aids.

lisp-implementation-type	get-decoded-time
lisp-implementation-version	dribble
machine-type	load
machine-version	room
machine-instance	describe
software-type	inspect
software-version	compile
short-site-name	time
long-site-name	sleep
internal-time-units-per-second	step

LESSON 7
Output and Strings, *72*
    Using output functions and strings. Binding within functions.

stringp	boundp
princ	let
format (using ~% and ~<RET>)	labels
terpri	>

LESSON 8
The Read, Evaluate and Output Loop, *86*
    Reading, evaluating and returning expressions.
    read
    eval
    type-of

LESSON 9
Parameter Passing, *95*
    Optional and rest parameters.
    &optional
    &rest

LESSON 10
Controlling Execution Flow (2), *106*
    Loop control structures, return and case functions.
dolist	loop
dotimes	return
do	case

LESSON 11
Using Functions, *123*
    Functions as parameters and data objects. Lambda functions.
apply	functionp
funcall	function
mapcar	#'
maplist	lambda

LESSON 12
List Manipulation (3), *133*
    Even more functions for working with lists (and other sequences).
adjoin	subseq
butlast	union
count	intersection
elt	subsetp
find	delete
last	substitute
member	find-if
position	position-if
remove	count-if
remove-duplicates	delete-duplicates
sort	

LESSON 13
Program Constructs, *145*
    Functions to structure functions and define scope.
block	catch
return-from	throw
tagbody	prog
go	

LESSON 14
Streams, *159*
    Creating and manipulating streams.
close	input-stream-p
make-string-input-stream	make-synonym-stream
make-string-output-stream	stream-element-type
streamp	y-or-n-p
get-output-stream-string	yes-or-no-p
output-stream-p	

LESSON 15
Files, *169*

Opening, closing, reading and writing files.

file-position	read-char
file-length	read-line
open	unread-char
peek-char	with-open-file
pprint	write
prin1	y-or-no-p

LESSON 16
Association and Property Lists, *180*

acons	symbol-plist
assoc	rassoc
get	consp
remprop	equal

LESSON 17
Equality, *193*

eq	char=
eql	char-equal
equal	string=
equalp	string-equal
=	

LESSON 18
Characters and Strings, *199*

char	character
char=	char-equal
char/=	char-not-equal
char<	char-lessp
char>	char-greaterp
char<=	char-not-greaterp
char>=	char-not-lessp
char-downcase	char-upcase
char-int	code-char
digit-char-p	lower-case-p
string=	string-equal
string/=	string-not-equal
string<	string-lessp
string>	string-greaterp
string<=	string-not-greaterp
string>=	string-not-lessp
string-capitalize	string-downcase
string-upcase	upper-case-p
standard-char-p	graphic-char-p
alpha-char-p	alphanumericp
upper-case-p	lower-case-p
both-case-p	digit-char-p
char-code-limit	string

CONTENTS

    make-string
    string-left-trim
    length
    reverse
    subseq
    elt
    concatenate
    remove

    string-trim
    string-right-trim
    delete
    substitute
    position
    count
    find
    sort

LESSON 19
Numbers, *210*

    /
    integerp
    rationalp
    floatp
    plusp
    minusp
    oddp
    evenp
    =
    /=
    <
    >
    <=
    >=
    exp
    expt
    log

    sqrt
    sin
    cos
    abs
    pi
    float
    rational
    numerator
    denominator
    floor
    ceiling
    truncate
    round
    incf
    decf
    random

LESSON 20
Arrays, *225*

    aref
    array-dimension
    array-dimensions
    arrayp
    vectorp
    array-rank

    make-array
    vector
    array-total-size
    array-rank-limit
    array-dimension-limit
    array-total-size-limit

LESSON 21
Structures, *235*

    defstruct
    make-
    copy-

PREFACE

The best kind of learning is learning by doing. This book is intended to provide you an opportunity to learn Common Lisp by actually working with it.

Common Lisp is the standard version of Lisp and is an increasingly important language for computing. It is a very large and powerful language. (The standard reference for it, **Common Lisp The Language**, by Guy Steele, is about 1,000 pages long.) This book does not cover all of the features of Common Lisp. Enough Common Lisp is covered to make you comfortable with it and so that almost any feature of Common Lisp resembles one you have already seen. (This turns out to be quite a lot!)

I have had a lot of fun programming in Lisp and I expect that you will as well.

Although a person with no background in programming could use this book, that person would miss a great deal. You should have had programming experience in some other language (e.g. Pascal). In particular, you should have some acquaintance with things like variables, data structures, files, control structures and subprograms, including recursive subprograms. Your appreciation of these will be enhanced by the work you do in Lisp. On the other hand, don't expect programming in Lisp to be much like programming in other languages. It isn't.

A word about the book's organization. The Preliminaries (about things you need to know to use the book) should be done first. Lessons 1 through 10 should be done in order and before any of the remaining lessons. Lessons 11 through 21 are more or less independent of one another. Furthermore, within each of lessons 11 through 21 the most important part occurs first. Consequently, if time is limited, just doing the first part of these will be beneficial.

The Department of Mathematics and Computer Science at Bloomsburg University gave me opportunities which made this book possible and I am grateful to and indebted to my colleagues. I am even more indebted to my students who used preliminary versions of it. They have educated me more than I have educated them. I also am grateful to Prentice-Hall for their support and assistance in bringing this project to fruition. Finally, I would like to acknowledge the support my family has given me while I have been writing this.

DEDICATED TO MY STUDENTS

PRELIMINARIES

INTRODUCTION

This book is designed to familiarize you with the programming language Common Lisp by actually working in it. Most of the book consists of procedures for you to follow using Common Lisp. But before this is possible, we need to cover some preliminary material. In this chapter, we outline some things you need to know in order to use Common Lisp and the computer system. We also describe the format and conventions of the lessons.

Common Lisp is a standard (or perhaps standardized) language. This means that all implementations of Common Lisp work the same and that it is possible for us to write about it precisely. (Actually, much of the material covered is present in other versions of Lisp, but usually with minor variations.)

As a matter of convenience, we'll usually use the term "Lisp" instead of "Common Lisp."

Unfortunately, the environments (the hardware and operating systems) in which Lisp runs can vary. Consequently, there is some system information which the Lisp programmer must know but we are unable to describe in this text. You will have to find them out from an instructor, a friend, a book, or, as a last resort, the system manuals.

In this section, we describe, albeit in vague generality, some procedures which you must know and some others which are useful. If you are familiar with the system, most of this will be known to you. If you are not, we suggest that you write down essential information.

Don't feel that you need to memorize this all at once. In fact, you won't need to know everything when you start. Things you must know to get started begin with a triple asterisk (***). Other items, which are useful but not immediately essential, are preceded by a triple dash (— — —). As you use the system, you will no longer need to refer to your notes, but it's a good idea to have them.

USING THE SYSTEM

In order to use Lisp, you must be able to access a computer. Getting on the computer may be as simple as pressing an ON/OFF switch (e.g., a personal computer). If you are using a multiuser system, this will be a bit more complicated and almost certainly involve a user identification and password. Answer the questions that pertain to your situation.

∗∗∗ How does one physically access the computer system? What switches must be turned on? Are there switch settings that need to be set? Is access via a modem or a network? If so, how?

In other words, how does one establish a communication with the computer?

∗∗∗ Once a physical connection has been established, it may be necessary to identify yourself to the system. A common way of doing this is via a user ID and password. If this is the case, you must obtain an ID and password from the powers that be. You probably will need to change your password from the one that is initially assigned. DO NOT WRITE YOUR PASSWORD DOWN. The process of identifying yourself to the computer is known as *logging on*. What are the steps to logging on to your system?

∗∗∗ When you are done using the computer, what do you do? In a multiuser system, there generally is a *logoff* or *logout* procedure. What is it? When you finish, make sure you use it. Never leave access to anything you value.

— — — Most operating systems organize things to be saved into files. (The storage mechanism may not be termed "files." We will use the term "file." You may substitute whatever is comparable on your system.) Usually there are conventions for naming files. What are they? How many characters (letters, digits, and so on) are permitted in a file name? Eventually, you may want to take advantage of ways of grouping the files. (A group of files is frequently called a *directory*.) There also may be ways of specifying a group of files, using so-called *matchall* or *wildcard characters*. Is this possible using your system and, if so, how?

— — — Here is a list of things that might be done with a file. Find out whether each is possible on your system and, if so, how. ("How" means the actions or commands necessary to achieve the result.)

Eliminate (erase, delete, remove, trash, and so forth) a file.

Make an archival (or backup) copy of a file.

Copy a file to external storage (probably a floppy disk; what size, what density, what format?)

Rename a file.

Print the contents of the file.

— — — How can you modify the contents of the file? Typically, modification is done using a program called an *editor* or a *word processor*. Learning to use an editor or word processor well is usually time consuming and tedious. Unless you know you are going to use the system a lot or know the word processor is going to be used elsewhere, don't bother trying to learn all its details. Just learn the minimum you need: how to enter and delete text at different points in the file.

PRELIMINARIES

RUNNING LISP

Lisp is an *interpreted language*. This means that once you start the Lisp system, it can be considered "self-contained." Lisp must be started somehow.

*** How do you start the Lisp interpreter? A common way of doing this is just by typing "LISP" or "lisp" (at the system prompt).

*** How do you stop a "runaway" Lisp process (e.g., an *infinite loop*)? Pressing the break key or a "control key" may do it. What are the consequences of doing this? This may be a very drastic step.

*** What happens if you make an error using Lisp? Most versions of Lisp start an *error-handling routine*. What must you do to continue working once the error-handling starts? You'll probably only need to type one or two things. In fact, the Lisp system may inform you of possible responses. Be forewarned, to make certain points, we have deliberately written things that should cause errors. (Of course, there may be other errors.)

*** How do you end a Lisp session and return to the operating system? Entering "(quit)," "(exit)," or "(system)" may work. The parentheses are probably needed.

LISP CONVENTIONS

The rest of this book consists of lessons to be completed using Lisp. When Lisp starts, it will output a message. When Lisp is ready, a *prompt* (a symbol indicating the system is waiting for input) will appear. At this point, the Lisp programmer enters what is known as an *expression*. After the expression has been entered, the Lisp system evaluates it and returns its value.

For example, if the Lisp prompt is > and the programmer entered "(+ 2 3)" (usually followed by a return or enter) the Lisp system would output 5 (the value of "(+ 2 3)") and then a prompt (indicating Lisp is ready for another expression). This would appear as follows (where (+ 2 3) <RET> is entered by the programmer).

```
>  (+ 2 3)
5
```

Each lesson contains Lisp expressions which you are to have Lisp evaluate. As you do this you should pay attention to what Lisp does. Expressions to enter are preceded by a prompt, the greater than symbol (>). (Your system may use a different prompt.) Expressions may extend over more than one line. A blank line follows each expression to be entered. (You may want to write down what Lisp returns here.) For example, to indicate you are to enter (+ 2 3) (followed by a return), the following would appear in a lesson:

> (+ 2 3)

We have generally written Lisp expressions to be entered in lower case letters. Lisp may return values in upper case. In discussing Lisp, Lisp language elements and Lisp code are in bold type. As a consequence, we would write "defun" in code, as in "(defun f(x) (* x x))" and "**defun**" in a question or commentary as in "What is the purpose of **defun**?"

Lisp expressions frequently involve lots of parentheses. (An old quip is that Lisp stands for *L*ots of *I*rritating *S*ingle *P*arentheses.) It is important to enter expressions and their parentheses correctly. Every left parenthesis must be matched with a right parenthesis. Parenthesized expressions may occur within one another. They may also extend over more than one line.

To make Lisp easier to read and emphasize which expressions occur within which, we will write Lisp expressions using the following conventions. If an expression within an expression needs to be put on a separate line, the inside expression will be indented. The right parenthesis which matches a left parenthesis will either be on the same line or directly below it (on a line by itself). For example (don't worry about the meaning of this),

> (defun f(x)
    (cond
        ((numberp x) (* x x))
        (t (list x))
)
)

The last right parenthesis matches the first left parenthesis (before **defun**) and the next to last right parenthesis matches the left parenthesis preceding **cond**. The middle two lines, **((numberp x) (* x x))** and **(t (list x))**, are expressions which fit on one line. Notice that on these two lines every left parenthesis is matched by a right parenthesis. These two expressions occur within the expression that starts with **(cond** so they are indented. Similarly, since **(cond ...** is contained within the expression that begins with **(defun** it is indented.

Incidentally, Lisp expressions frequently end with a group of right parentheses. (In the preceding example, there were four. More than four are entirely possible.) A common style is to put these all at the end, on one line. We have not done this so that the matching of parentheses is easier to see.

A Lisp comment begins with a semicolon (;) and extends rightward to the end of the line. That is, anything to the right of a semicolon (including the semicolon itself) is ignored by Lisp. Occasionally, a comment will appear to the right of a Lisp expression as an explanatory note as in this example.

> (setf n-l '((a b c d)))   ; Nested List

In the lessons, there are instructions and questions for you to follow and answer. Instructions and questions are distinguished from the Lisp you are to enter by being indented and by being printed in a different typeface. For example, in the following lines, you are to enter **(+ 2 3)** and see what happens and then answer the question "What is the value of the following Lisp expression?" (The Lisp expression is **(+ 7 8)**.)

Enter the following.

> (+ 2 3)

What is the value of the following Lisp expression?

(+ 7 8)

Occasionally, it is necessary to be emphatic about something. To call special attention, we use a comment which starts with two semicolons and two asterisks as illustrated.

;; ** DANGER, SHARP CURVE AHEAD

In a sense, Lisp remembers what has been entered during a session. Most of the time, a lesson depends on what has already been entered during the lesson. As a matter of convenience, within each lesson there are places at which the lesson can be interrupted. You can quit working at such a point and resume at a later time. These break points are marked (as below) by a solid horizontal line which have a blank line before and after.

That is, the part of the lesson which follows the break point does not depend upon the part which precedes the break point.

Throughout the lessons there are questions you are to answer. Two types of questions frequently occur.

The question "What is the value of the following expression?" (or something similar) means that you are to give the value that Lisp would return if the expression was entered. Most of the time the answer should be obvious. You can double check your answer simply by entering the expression to Lisp.

The question "Give an expression which has the value **X**." means that you are to write an expression which will evaluate to **X**.

Like English, there may be more than one way of expressing the same thing in Lisp. An exercise of the form "Express **X** using **Y** and **Z**." means that you are to write an expression using **Y** and **Z** which always has exactly the same value as **X**.

In some lessons, it is useful to give examples of the value that is to be returned by something you have written. The symbol => is used to indicate that expression to the left of => is to produce the value on the right. In the following, **(double 7)** => **14** indicates that when **(double 7)** is evaluated it should produce the value **14**.

Write a function **double** which ...
...
For example,

(double 7) => **14**

You should implement and test things you have written. In the preceding, after you have written **double** you should enter **(double 7)** and see what happens.

Each Lisp lesson ends with a brief summary.

Finally, we encourage you to "experiment" or "play" with Lisp. Don't limit yourself to the lessons. If you wonder what will happen if ...? Try it and find out. You can learn a lot by trying things and seeing what Lisp does. Have some fun!

LESSON 1
Using Lisp

Enter the following expressions and note the values that are returned. (Recall that > denotes the Lisp prompt and that expressions are followed by a return.)

> `(+ 2 3)`

> `(+ 2 3 4)`

> `(+ 2 4 6 8)`

> `(+ 3)`

> `(+ )`

> `(+ 001 0002)`

> `(+ 1000`
  `2200`
  `3330`
  `4444`
  `)`

> `(- 3 2)`

> `(- 9 3 4)`

> (− 20 1 2 3 4 5)

> (− 8)

> (−)

What is the value of each of the following expressions? (Recall this means what value will Lisp return when the expression is evaluated?)

(+ 4 5)

(+ 7)

(+ 3 4 5)

(− 7 3)

(− 10 1 3 5)

Give an expression for the sum of 33 and 55.

Give an expression for the sum of 1000 and 99999999.

Give an expression for the difference of 77 and 22.

Give an expression for the sum of the numbers 2 through 8 (inclusive).

Give an expression which returns the result of subtracting the numbers 5 through 9 from 50.

Describe what + does.

Describe what − does.

Enter the following expressions and note the value that is returned.

LESSON 1   3

> (− (+ 4 5) 6)

> (− (+ 10 20) (+ 3 7))

> (+ (− 10 5) (− 12 8))

> (+ (− 9 4) (− 4 3) (− 7 1))

> (− (+ 2 4 6 8) (+ 1 2 3))

> (− (+ (− 7 2) (− 3 1)) (− 10 4))

What are the values of the following expressions?

(− (+ 2 3 4) (+ 1 2))

(+ (− 10 5) (+ 4 6))

Give an expression which returns the difference of the sum of the numbers 10 through 14 subtracted from the sum of the numbers 12 through 18.

Describe what happened in the above. Compare with your descriptions of + − given prior to entering the expressions. Revise your descriptions of + − if necessary.

Enter the following expressions and note the values that are returned.

> (quote x)

> (quote hello)

> (quote go)

> (quote (a b c d e))

> (quote ((a b) (c d)))

> (quote 8)

> (quote (+ 2 4))

> (quote (+ 2 3 4))

> (quote (− (+ 12 8) 7))

> (quote (quote x))

What are the values of the following expressions?

(+ 20 30 40)

(quote (+ 20 30 40))

Write an expression whose value is the expression (* 10 20 30).

Describe what **quote** does.

Enter the following expressions and note the values that are returned.

> 'x   ; ' is the single quote or apostrophe.

> 'hello

> 'goodbye

> '(a b c d e)

> '((a b) (c d))

> '8

> '(+ 2 3)

> '(+ 2 3 4)

> '(− (+ 12 8) 7)

> '(quote x)

LESSON 1

> ''x

Compare your answers with the answers you obtained using **quote**. What do you conclude?

Because it's more convenient, we'll use ' not **quote**.

Enter the following.

> (setf greeting 'hello)

> greeting

> 'greeting

> (setf a-list '(a b c d e))

> a-list

> 'a-list

> (setf nested-list '((a b) (c d)))

> nested-list

> 'nested-list

> z

> (setf z 0)

> z

> (setf iv 4)

> iv

> (+ iv 5)

> (* 2 iv)

> (+ iv ix)

> (setf ix 9)

> (+ iv ix)

> (* iv ix)

What do each of the following do?

(setf farewell 'goodbye)

(setf long-list '(a b c d e f g h i j k l m n))

(setf x 10)

Write an expression which assigns the value **hi** to the variable **another-greeting**. That is, entering **another-greeting** at the prompt should cause **hi** to be returned.

Write an expression which assigns the value **11** to the variable **xi**.

Write an expression which returns the double of **xi**.

Write an expression which returns four more than **xi**.

Enter the following and note what happens.

> (setf a-sum (+ 2 3))

> a-sum

> (setf triple-sum (* 3 a-sum))

> triple-sum

> (setf not-a-sum '(+ 2 3))

> not-a-sum

> (* 4 not-a-sum)

Explain what happened in the preceding. In particular, what is the difference between the expressions using **setf** with **a-sum** and **not-a-sum**?

LESSON 1

Enter the following.

> (setf vii (+ 1 (setf vi 6)))

> vii

> vi

Explain what happened when the preceding three expressions were evaluated.

Enter the following.

> (setq exclamation 'oh!)   ; Note: setq (Q) not setf (F)

> exclamation

> (setq twenty (* 2 (setq ten 10)))

> twenty

> ten

What caused **ten** and **twenty** to have the values returned in the preceding?

Using the variables just given values (i.e. **ten** and **twenty**) write expressions which give **thirty** and **one-hundred** appropriate values.

At this point, can you tell the difference between **setf** and **setq**?

Enter the following.

> a

> 'a

> A

> 'A

> #\A

> #\a

> (setq big-a #\A)

> big-a

> (setq little-a #\a)

> little-a

> (setq #\a 'alpha)

> (setq two #\2)

> two

> (+ two two)

What is returned when the following are evaluated?

#\M

#\m

#\7

What is the difference between **a**, **'a** and **#\a** ?

SUMMARY

Arithmetic operators (+ − *) precede their operands (numbers to be added, subtracted, multiplied). The expression to be evaluated must be enclosed in parentheses. These expressions may be nested.

The function **quote** prevents the expression that follows it from being evaluated. The apostrophe (') is equivalent to **quote**.

The functions **setq** and **setf** are used to give a variable a value.

Characters are given using a pound-backslash combination (#\ ) .

LESSON 2
List Manipulation (1)

Enter the following. Note the values returned when using **first** and **rest**.

> (first '(hammer saw pliers))

> (first '(screwdriver))

> (first '(4 5 6 7 8))

> (rest '(hammer saw pliers))

> (rest '(4 5 6 7 8))

> (setf tools '(hammer saw pliers))

> (first tools)

> (rest tools)

> (setq more-tools '(wrench drill vice knife))

> (first more-tools)

> (rest more-tools)

> (first (rest tools))

LESSON 2

> (rest (rest tools))

> (first (first tools))

> (first (rest more-tools))

> (rest (rest more-tools))

What is returned by the following expressions?

(first '(x y z))

(rest '(x y z))

(first (rest '(alpha beta delta gamma)))

(rest (rest '(alpha beta delta gamma)))

Write an expression using **first** and **'(m n o p)** which returns the symbol **M**.

Write an expression using **rest** and **'(m n o p)** which returns the list **(N O P)**.

Write an expression using **first**, **rest** and **'(m n o p)** which returns the symbol **N**.

Write an expression using **rest** and **'(m n o p)** which returns the list **(O P)**.

Write an expression using **first**, **rest** and the list **'(10 20 30 40)** which returns the value **10**.

Write an expression using **first**, **rest** and the list **'(10 20 30 40)** which returns the list **(20 30 40)**.

LIST MANIPULATION (1)

Write an expression using **first**, **rest** and the list **'(10 20 30 40)** which returns the list **(30 40)**.

Write an expression using **first**, **rest** and the list **'(10 20 30 40)** which returns the value **30**.

Enter the following.

> ()

> nil

> (first '(one-thing))

> (rest '(one-thing))

> (   )

> '( )

What does **nil** signify?

Give a list which has the value **nil**.

Enter the following.

> (rest ())

> (first ())

> (rest nil)

> (first nil)

> (first '(one-item))

> (rest '(one-item))

LESSON 2

What is **first** of an empty list?

What is **rest** of an empty list?

What is **rest** of a list with one item?

What is the value of **(rest (rest '(one-thing another-thing)))**?

Write an expression using **rest** and **'(10 20 30)** which has the value **nil**.

Enter the following and note what is returned.

> (first (setf shopping-list '(eggs ham bacon flour pepper salt)))
> shopping-list
> (rest (rest shopping-list))

Explain the values that were returned by the preceding preceding three expressions.

Enter the following and note what is returned.

> (setf n-l '((a b c) (x y z) (1 2 3)))   ; n-l for nested list
> (first n-l)
> (rest n-l)

> (first (first n-l))

> (first (rest n-l))

> (rest (first n-l))

Answer the following questions using **n-l** as defined above. What is the value of each of the following?

(rest (rest n-l))

(rest (rest (first n-l)))

(first (rest (rest n-l)))

Write an expression using **first**, **rest** and **n-l** which returns the value **B**.

Enter the following and note what is returned.

> (setf n-n-l '(a (b (c (d e)))))   ; n-n-l for nested nested list

> (first n-n-l)

> (rest n-n-l)

> (rest (rest n-n-l))

> (first (rest n-n-l))

Write an expression using **first**, **rest** and **n-n-l** which returns **(C (D E))**.

Write a description of what **first** does.

Write a description of what **rest** does.

LESSON 2

Enter the following. Note the effect of **second**.

> (second '(cobol fortran pascal))

> (second '(lisp prolog))

> (second '(apl))

> (setf a-list '((a b c) (x y z)))

> (second a-list)

> (first (second a-list))

> (second (rest a-list))

> (second (first (rest a-list)))

Using the value of **a-list** defined above what values are returned by the following?

(second (second a-list))

(second (first a-list))

(rest (second a-list))

Describe what **second** does in terms of **first** and **rest**.

Enter the following, noting what is returned.

> (cons 'a nil)   ; **cons** for CONStruct.

> (cons 'a '(b))

> (cons 'a '(b c))

LIST MANIPULATION (1)

> (cons 'a (cons 'b nil))

> (cons 'a (cons 'b   '(c d)))

> (cons 'a (cons 'b (cons 'c nil)))

> (cons '(a) '(b))

> (cons '(a b) '(c d))

> (setf a 'alpha)

> (setf b 'beta)

> (cons a nil)

> (cons a (cons b nil))

> (setf primaries (cons 'red '(yellow blue)))

> primaries

> (first primaries)

> (rest primaries)

> (setf secondaries (cons 'green ()))

> secondaries

> (first secondaries)

> (rest secondaries)

> (setf secondaries (cons 'orange secondaries))

> secondaries

> (setf secondaries (cons 'purple secondaries))

> secondaries

> (setf colors (cons primaries secondaries))

> (first colors)

> (rest colors)

> (cons 'white colors)

LESSON 2

> colors

> (cons (first primaries) (rest primaries))

> primaries

> (cons (+ 1 2) '(10 20))

> (cons (* 3 4) '(+ 30 40))

What are the values of the following?

(cons 'and-a '(one))

(cons 'and-a (cons 'one '(and-a two)))

Suppose L has been assigned the value '(a b c). Write expressions using **cons**, L and possibly **first** or **rest** which have the values '(1 a b c), '(x y a b c), '((a b c) a b c) and '(x b c).

Suppose **something** is a Lisp object and **some-list** is a list and the following expression is entered.

(setf another-list (cons something some-list))

What are **(first another-list)** and **(rest another-list)**?

Describe what **cons** does. Relate **cons** to **first** and **rest**.

Enter the following, where **colors** is the list already constructed. Note the values of **colors** and **basics**.

> (setf basics '(black white))

> (setf colors (cons basics colors))

> colors

> basics

> (setf basics (cons 'gray basics))

> colors

> basics

What can you conclude about the value of a list which has been used in constructing another list? Does it remain unchanged?

Enter the following. Contrast **car** and **cdr** (pronounced "coulder") with **first** and **rest**.

> (car '(hammer saw pliers))

> (car '(screwdriver))

> (car '(4 5 6 7 8))

> (cdr '(hammer saw pliers))

> (cdr '(4 5 6 7 8))

> (setf tools '(hammer saw pliers))

> (car tools)

> (cdr tools)

> (setq more-tools '(wrench drill vice knife))

> (car more-tools)

> (cdr more-tools)

> (car (cdr tools))

LESSON 2

> (cdr (cdr tools))

> (car (car tools))

> (car (cdr more-tools))

> (cdr (cdr more-tools))

What are the values of the following expresssions?

(car '(x y z))

(cdr '(x y z))

(car (cdr '(alpha beta delta gamma)))

(cdr (cdr '(alpha beta delta gamma)))

Use **car** and **cdr** with the list **'(m n o p q)** to write expressions with the values **M**, **(N O P Q)**, **N** and **(O P Q)**.

Use **car** and **cdr** with the list **'((1 2 3) (10 9 8))** to write expressions which have the values **2** and value **10**.

What are **car** and **cdr** in terms of **first** and **rest**?

Enter the following and note the results that are returned. Assume **tools** and **more-tools** are defined as above.

> (cadr tools)

> (cadr more-tools)

> (cddr tools)

> (cddr more-tools)

> (setf tool-lists (cons tools (cons more-tools ())))

> (cadr tool-lists)

> (cddr tool-lists)

> (caar tool-lists)

> (cdar tool-lists)

What are the values of the following expressions?

(cadr '(10 20 30 40))

(cddr '(10 20 30 40))

(cadr '((a b c) (d e f) (h i j)))

(cdar '((a b c) (d e f) (h i j)))

(caar '((a b c) (d e f) (h i j)))

(cddr '((a b c) (d e f) (h i j)))

caar, **cadr**, **cdar**, **cddr** are abbreviations for combinations of **car** and **cdr**. Tell what each of **caar**, **cadr**, **cdar**, **cddr** does in terms of **car** and **cdr**.

One of **caar**, **cadr**, **cdar**, **cddr** corresponds to **second**. Which one?

SUMMARY

A list is a group of objects enclosed in parentheses. (Objects within a list can be lists yielding nested lists.) A list with no items is called the empty list is denoted **nil**.

The function **first** returns the first item of a list. The function **rest** returns a list with its first item removed. The second item of a list is obtained using **second**.

The function **cons** constructs a list from an object and a list.

The functions **car** and **cdr** are old (but often used) names for **first** and **rest**. The functions **caar**, **cadr**, **cdar** and **cddr** are combinations of **car** and **cdr**.

LESSON 3
Defining Functions

Enter the following. Recall that an indented line is a continuation of the expression on the preceding line (or lines).

> (defun double (x) (* 2 x))   ; defun for DEfine FUNction

> (double 4)

> (double 3.5)

> (double (+ 3 4))

> (double (double 10))

> (+ (double 100) 3)

> (defun quad (x) (double (double x)))   ; quad for QUADruple

> (quad 9)

> (quad (double 3))

> (+ (quad 5) (double 6))

> (defun triple&add (x y) (+ (* 3 x) y))

LESSON 3

> (triple&add 4 5)

> (triple&add (+ 1 2) 7)

> (triple&add (double 5) 8)

> (triple&add (triple&add 2 3) (triple&add 4 5))

> (defun head (l) (car l))

> (head '(a b c))

> (setf groceries '(milk juice lettuce carrots rice))

> (head groceries)

> (defun tail (l) (cdr l))

> (tail groceries)

> (head (tail groceries))

> (setf dairy-product (head groceries))

> dairy-product

> (defun list-build (something a-list)   ; something is added to a-list
           (cons something a-list)
)

> (list-build 1 '(2 3 4))

> (list-build 'junk nil)

> (setf dairy-list (list-build dairy-product ()))

> dairy-list

> (setf dairy-list (list-build 'cheese dairy-list))

> dairy-list

What is returned when each of the following expressions is entered?

(defun add10 (x) (+ x 10))

(add10 3)

(add10 (+ 2 3))

(add10 (add10 9))

(defun add20 (x) (add10 (add10 x)))

(add20 8)

(add20 (add10 0))

(defun remove-second (l) (cons (car l) (cddr l)))

(remove-second '(a b c d))

(remove-second '((a b) (c d)))

(remove-second '(a b))

(remove-second (remove-second '(a b c d e f)))

(remove-second '(a))   ; This one and the next one are a little subtle.

(remove-second ())

Write an expression which makes **cube** a function which returns the cube of a number. For example,

(cube 2) => **8**

Make sure your function works by trying it with a few values.

Write an expression which makes **remove-third** a function which returns a list which is the list supplied without its third element. For example,

(remove-third '(a b c d e f)) => **(A B D E F)**

Implement and test your function.

What is the purpose of **defun**?

LESSON 3

Enter the following.

```
> t                              ; for True
> T
> (numberp 10)
> (numberp 'a)
> (numberp '(1))
> (numberp (+ 1 2))
> (setf xii 12)
> (numberp xii)
> (symbolp 'a)
> (symbolp 20)
> (symbolp '(1 2 3))
> (symbolp xii)
> (symbolp 'xii)
> (setf autos '(sedan convertible station-wagon))
> (symbolp autos)
> (symbolp 'autos)
> (symbolp (car autos))
> (symbolp (cdr autos))
> (symbolp ())
> (symbolp nil)
> (symbolp (symbolp autos))
```

> (symbolp t)

> (symbolp 12)

> (symbolp '12)

> (null ())

> (null autos)

> (null 9)

> (null 'a)

> (null (cdr '(one-item)))

> (null (cdr autos))

> (null (cdddr autos))

> (null (cddddr autos))

> (null (car autos))

> (listp '(a b c))

> (listp ())

> (listp nil)

> (listp autos)

> (listp (cdr autos))

> (listp (car autos))

> (listp 'a)

> (listp 12)

> (listp (+ 2 3))

What is the value (**t** or **nil**) of each of the following?

(numberp 9)

(numberp 'seven)

LESSON 3

(numberp '(100 200))

(numberp (+ 100 200))

(numberp '(+ 100 200))

(numberp (numberp 2))

(symbolp 9)

(symbolp 'nine)

(symbolp '(eight nine ten))

(symbolp (car '(eight nine ten)))

(symbolp (cdr '(eight nine ten)))

(symbolp (numberp 8))

(null '(eight nine ten))

(null (car '(eight nine ten)))

(null (cdr '(eight nine ten)))

(null (cdddr '(eight nine ten)))

(listp 9)

(listp 'nine)

(listp '(eight nine ten))

(listp (car '(eight nine ten)))

(listp (cdr '(eight nine ten)))

(listp (cdddr '(eight nine ten)))

numberp, **symbolp**, **null** and **listp** are called predicates. (That's what the suffix p represents.) Describe what each of them does.

In general, what does a predicate do?

Enter the following.

> (cond
      ((numberp 9) "A number")
      (t   "Not a number")
)

> (cond
      ((numberp 'a) "A number")
      (t   "Not a number")
)

> (cond
      ((numberp 'a) "A number")
      ((symbolp 'a) "A symbol")
      (t   "Not a number or a symbol")
)

> (cond
      ((symbolp 'a) "A symbol")
      ((numberp 'a) "A number")
      (t   "Not a number or symbol.")
)

> (defun classify (x)
      (cond
          ((null x) "Empty list")
          ((listp x) "Nonempty list")
          ((symbolp x) "A symbol")

```
                ((numberp x) "A number")
                (t "What's this?")
        )
    )
> (classify 'a)
> (classify 9)
> (classify 9/2)
> (classify 9.5)
> (classify 9.5e2)
> (classify ())
> (classify (+ 3 4 5))
> (classify '(+ 3 4 5))
> (classify '(a b c))
> (classify '((a b) (c d)))
> (classify (car '(1 2 3)))
> (classify (cdddr '(a b c)))
> (classify #\A)
> (classify #\8)
> (classify "Hello")
> (classify '("Hello" "Goodbye"))
> (classify (car '("Hello" "Goodbye")))
> (classify (classify '(a b c)))
> (defun classify-list (x)
        (cond
            ((null x) "An empty list")
            ((listp x) "A nonempty list")
            (t "Not a list")
        )
    )
```

> (classify-list 9)

> (classify-list ())

> (classify '(a b c))

> (defun reclassify-list (x)
      (cond
          ((listp x) "A list")
          ((null x) "An empty list")
          (t "What's this?")
)
)

> (reclassify-list 9)

> (reclassify-list '(a b c))

> (reclassify-list ())

> (reclassify-list (cdr ()))

> (defun check&double (n)
      (cond
          ((numberp n) (* 2 n))
          (t   n)
)
)

> (check&double 8)

> (check&double '(a b c))

> (check&double (car '(4 x y z)))

> (check&double (cdr '(4 x y z)))

> (check&double (car '(x y z 4)))

> (check&double (+ 3 4))

> (defun first-symbol (x)
      (cond
          ((null x) ())
          ((symbolp x) x)
          ((symbolp (car x)) (car x))
          (t "First symbol not found")
)
)

LESSON 3

> (first-symbol '(a b c))

> (first-symbol 'a)

> (first-symbol '(1 2 3 x y z))

> (first-symbol ())

> (first-symbol '((x y z) a b c))

Consider the function **f** defined as follows.

```
(defun f (x)
    (cond
        ((null x) "Hello")
        ((numberp x) (* 10 x))
        ((listp x) (car x))
        (t "Goodbye")
    )
)
```

What is returned by each of the following?

(f 2)
(f ())
(f '(a b c))
(f (f 4))
(f 'Hello)
(f '((a b c) (d e f)))
(f (f '(3 4 5)))

Describe what **f** does.

Will the function **reclassify-list** ever return the value "**An empty list**"? Why or why not?

Describe the difference between the functions **classify-list** and **reclassify-list** that were defined above. What does this imply about **cond**?

Each of the expressions which follows **cond** is called a clause. (For example, the clauses in the **cond** of **classify-list** are

((listp x) "A list")
((null x)   "An empty list")
(t "What's this?")))

What would be the effect of starting the first clause of a **cond** with **t**?

Write a function which, when applied to a number returns the triple of the number and when applied to a nonempty list returns the first object of the list. When the function is applied to any other value it should return the value. Implement and test the function.

Describe what **cond** does.

The next few lines are an aside. **1+** is handy.

Enter the following.

> (1+ 7)

> (1+ (* 2 10))

What does **1+** do?

>   ; Here's where the fun begins.

Enter the following.

LESSON 3

```
> (defun count-symbols (x)
      (cond
          ((null (listp x)) 0)
          ((null x) 0)
          ((symbolp (car x)) (1+ (count-symbols (cdr x))))
          (t (count-symbols (cdr x)))
      )
  )

> (count-symbols '(a b c))

> (count-symbols '(a b c 3 4 x y z))

> (count-symbols '(1 a 2 b (c d)))

> (count-symbols '(1 2 3 (a b c) y))

> (count-symbols 1)

> (count-symbols ())

> (count-symbols '("Hello" hello hello))

> (defun count-all-symbols (x)
      (cond
          ((null x) 0)
          ((symbolp x) 1)
          ((listp x) (+ (count-all-symbols (car x))
                        (count-all-symbols (cdr x)))
          )
          (t 0)
      )
  )

> (count-all-symbols '(a b c 1 2))

> (count-all-symbols '((a b c) (1 2 3) (x y z)))

> (count-all-symbols '((a b) ((c d)))

> (count-all-symbols '(a (b (c (d (e))))))
```

Using the functions **count-symbols** and **count-all-symbols** just defined, give the values of the following.

(count-symbols (+ 1 2))

(count-symbols '(+ 1 2))

(count-symbols '(a b (c d)))

(count-all-symbols '(a b (c d)))

(count-symbols '(a 1 (b 2) (a 3)))

(count-all-symbols '(a 1 (b 2) (a 3)))

It's sometimes useful to see what's going on. Enter the following.

> (trace count-all-symbols)

> (count-all-symbols '(a b c))

> (count-all-symbols '((a b) (c d)))

> (untrace count-all-symbols)

> (count-all-symbols '(a b c))

Describe how **count-symbols** and **count-all-symbols** work. Note that **count-symbols** and **count-all-symbols** occur in their own definitions. (Such functions are called recursive.)

Write a function which returns the sum of the numbers in a list. Numbers in sublists should not be included in the sum. If the argument (the value given to the function) is not a list or the list is empty the function should return **0**. For example,

(list-sum '(2 a (3 5) 4 b)) $=>$ **6**

Write a function which returns the sum of all the numbers that occur in a list or lists within the list. If there are no numbers the function should return the value **0**. For example,

(all-list-sum '(2 a (3 5) 4 b)) $=>$ **14**

Use **trace** on the functions you have written.

SUMMARY

Defun is used to define functions. Roughly speaking, functions are the programs (and subprograms) of Lisp. A function may call itself (i.e. be recursive).

Predicates test for conditions and return the values **t** or **nil**. The predicates **numberp**, **symbolp** and **listp** test for the type of an object. **Null** tests for **nil**.

Cond evaluates a sequence of expressions and returns the value following the first expression which is not **nil**.

1+ returns one more than its argument.

Trace causes information about a function to be returned as it is evaluated.

LESSON 4
Controlling Execution Flow (1)

Enter the following.

> (eql 8 9)

> (eql 8 8)

> (eql 'a 'b)

> (eql 'a 'a)

>   ; Return a more meaningful message.

> (defun eql-test (x1 x2)
    (cond
        ((eql x1 x2)
            (format nil "~a and ~a are equal." x1 x2)
)
        (t   (format nil "~a and ~a are not equal." x1 x2))
)
)

> (eql-test 'A 'B)

> (eql-test 'a 'a)

LESSON 4

> (eql-test 'A 'a)

> (eql-test 1 1)

> (eql-test 1 2)

> (eql-test (* 10 10) 100)

> (eql-test 1 1.0)

> (eql-test 1 2/2)

> (eql-test 654321 654321)

> (eql-test 987654321 987654321)

> (eql-test 'a (car '(a b c)))

> (eql-test nil ())

> (eql-test t t)

> (eql-test t 'a)

> (eql-test t 't)

> (setq x 10)

> (setq ten 10)

> (eql-test x ten)

> (eql-test '(a b c) '(x y z))

> (eql-test '(a b c) '(a b c))

> (setq a-list '(a b c))

> (eql-test a-list '(a b c))

> (eql-test a-list a-list)

> (eql-test (car a-list) (car a-list)

> (eql-test (cdr a-list) (cdr a-list))

> (eql-test (cons 'z a-list) (cons 'z a-list))

> (setq another-list a-list)

> (eql-test a-list another-list)

> (setq yet-another-list (cons 'a (cdr a-list)))

> (eql-test a-list yet-another-list)

> (eql-test #\b #\b)

> (eql-test #\a #\A)

> (setq big-a #\A)

> (eql-test big-a #\A)

> (eql-test big-a #\a)

> (eql-test #\A 'a)

> (eql-test #\A 'A)

> (eql-test "Something" "Another thing")

> (eql-test "Something" "Something")

> (setq first-string "Hello")

> (setq second-string "Hello")

> (eql-test first-string second-string)

What are the values (**t** or **nil**) of the following expressions? (Assume they are entered without interruption.)

(eql 'A 'a)

(eql 12 (+ 4 2))

(eql 'u (car '(u v w x y z)))

(eql (+ 2 4 6) (+ 5 7))

(eql "Good" "Good")

(setf a-string "Good")

(eql a-string a-string)

LESSON 4   39

(eql a-string "Good")

(setf L1 '(a b c))

(setf L2 '(a b c))

(setf L3 L1)

(eql L1 L2)

(eql L1 L3)

(eql L2 L3)

Enter the following.

> (atom 9)

> (atom 'x)

> (atom nil)

> (atom '(a b c))

> (atom a-list)   ; a-list is already defined

> (atom (car a-list))

> (atom (cdr a-list))

>   ; Return a more meaningful message.

> (defun atom-test (x)
      (cond
          ((atom x) (format nil "~a is an atom." x))
          (t (format nil "~a is not an atom." x))
)
)

> (atom-test 4)

> (atom-test (+ 2 (* 3 4)))

> (atom-test a-list)

> (atom-test a-list)

> (atom-test (car a-list))

> (atom-test (cdr a-list))

> (atom-test (cadr a-list))

> (atom-test (cddr a-list))

> (atom-test (cdddr a-list))

> (atom-test "Something")

> (atom-test "Another thing")

What are the values of the following expressions? (Assume these are entered without interruption.)

(atom 'a)

(atom 9)

(atom (+ (* 3 4) (+ 2 5)))

(atom '(a b c))

(atom (setf LL '(e f g)))

(atom (car LL))

(atom (cdr LL))

A Lisp predicate for testing the type of a value (like **symbolp** and **listp**) is **stringp**. Write a few expressions to discover what it does.

The following predicates test whether an object is of a certain type. For each, describe the type (or types) for which the predicate returns **t**. Give examples of objects for which the predicate is true and not true.

symbolp

LESSON 4

    listp

    atom

    numberp

    stringp

    Describe what **eql** does.

Enter the following to discover what **not**, **or**, and **and** do. (Keep in mind that **in Lisp nil** is the equivalent of false.)

> `(not 'x)`

> `(not '(a b c))`

> (not 9)

> (not nil)

> (not nil)

> (not 'nil)

> (not ())

> (not "Hello there")

> (not (setf L '(a b c)))

> (not L)

> (not (car L))

> (not (cdddr L))

> (not 'a 'b)

> (defun not-null (x)   ; Do not and null do the same thing?
      (cond
           ((eql (null x) (not x))
                 (format nil "null, not same for ~a" x)
)
           (t   (format nil "null, not different for ~a" x))
)
)

> (not-null 'x)

> (not-null '(a b c))

> (not-null nil)

> (not-null 9)

> (not-null #\A)

> (not-null "A string")

What does **not** test for?

LESSON 4

Enter the following.

> (or 'a 'b 'c)
> (or nil 'a 'b 'c)
> (or 'a nil 'b 'c)
> (or '(a b c) '(x y z))
> (or nil '(x y z))
> (setf L '(a b c))
> (or (car L) (cadr L) (caddr L))
> (or (cdr L) (cddr L) (cdddr L))
> (or (cdddr L) (cddr L) (cdr L))
> (or (null L) (numberp L) (symbolp L))
> (or (null L) (listp L) (symbolp L))
> (and 'a 'b 'c)
> (and nil 'b nil)
> (and 'a 'b nil)
> (and '(a b c) '(x y z))
> (and (listp '(a b c)) (symbolp '(a b c)))
> (and (cdr L))
> (and (cdr L) (cddr L))
> (and (cdr L) (cddr L) (cdddr L))
> (and (car L) (cdr L) (cadr L))
> (or 1 2 3)
> (and 1 2 3)
> (or 1 2 3 4)

> **(and 1 2 3 4)**

What are the values of the following expressions?

(or '(a b) '(x y))

(and '(a b) '(x y))

(or nil '(x y))

(and nil '(x y))

(or '(a b) nil)

(and '(a b) nil)

(or 9 8 7)

(and 9 8 7)

(or nil 8 7)

(and nil 8 7)

(or 9 nil 7)

(and 9 nil 7)

Describe how **or** and **and** work and what they return.

If **a, b** and **c** are Lisp objects, express **(or a b c)** using **cond** (and possibly **t** or **nil**).

If **a, b** and **c** are Lisp objects, express **(and a b c)** using **cond** (and possibly **null, t,** or **nil**).

LESSON 4

Write a Lisp function which takes two arguments and returns **t** if the arguments are not lists and are the same (in the sense of **eql**) and **nil** otherwise. If both arguments are lists, the function is to return **t** if the corresponding objects in the lists, sublists, and so on are the same (in the sense of **eql**). If one argument is a list and the other is not, the function is to return **nil**. For example,

(equality '(a b c (d e)) '(a b c (d e))) => t

Implement and test your function.

Enter the following.

> (if t "Yes" "No")

> (if nil "Yes" "No")

> (if (not t) "Yes" "No")

> (if (not nil) "Yes" "No")

> (setf x 10)

> (if (numberp x) "A number" "Not a number")

> (if (listp x) "A list" "Not a list")

> (if 'a "Yes" "No")

> (if (not 'a) "Yes" "No")

> (setf L '(a b c))

> (if   L "Yes" "No")

> (if (car L) "Yes" "No")

> (if (cdr L) "Yes" "No")

> (if (cdddr L) "Yes" "No")

> (if (null (cdddr L)) "Yes" "No")

> (if 1 2 3)

> (if nil 2 3)

Give the values returned by the following.

(if 'a 'b 'c)

(if (listp '(a b c)) "A list" "Not a list")

(if (cdr '(a)) 'a "Empty")

(if (numberp 'a) 1 0)

(if (numberp (car '(9 a))) 1 0)

(if (numberp (cadr '(9 a))) 1 0)

Discover whether **if** works with two arguments. If it does describe what is returned.

Describe how **if** functions.

Express **(if x y z)** in terms of **cond**. (**T** must be used to do this.)

Write a function of two arguments which returns the sum of the two arguments if they are both numbers. If both arguments are not numbers the function is to return **0**. (An appropriate name for this is safe-add.) Use **if** and possibly **and** or **or**. For example,

(safe-add 2 3) => 5
(safe-add 2 '(a b c)) => 0

Write a function which returns a list of the sum of the corresponding numbers in two lists. If one list is longer than the other, the elements in the longer list are not used. For example, if the function is named **list-add**,

(list-add '(1 2 3) '(4 5 6 7)) => (4 7 9)

Use the function **safe-add** of the previous exercise for the addition so the function will work with lists that contain items other than numbers.

Enter the following.

> (zerop 0)

> (zerop 1)

What are the values of the following expressions?

(zerop 9)

(zerop (* 8 0))

(zerop '(a b c))

What does the predicate **zerop** test?

Enter the following.

> (when t (+ 2 3))

> (when nil (+ 2 3))

> (setf x 10)

> (when (numberp x) (princ x) (terpri) (* 2 x))

> (when (listp x) (princ (car c)) (terpri) (cdr x))

> (when t (princ 1) (terpri)
          (princ 2) (terpri)
          (princ 3) (terpri)
)

> (when nil (princ 1) (terpri)
            (princ 2) (terpri)
            (princ 3) (terpri)
)

> (defun when-ex1 (x)
      (when (not (zerop x)) (princ x) (terpri)
                            (when-ex1 (- x 1))
)
)

> (when-ex1 3)

LESSON 4

```
> (when-ex1 0)

> (when-ex1 1)

> (when-ex1 5)

> (defun when-ex2 (n)
    (when (oddp n)
        (princ (format nil "                    ~a" n))
        (terpri)
        (setf n (+ 1 (* 3 n)))
    )
    (when (evenp n)
        (princ (format nil "~a" n))
        (terpri)
        (setf n (/ n 2))
    )
    (when (not (equal n 1)) (when-ex2 n))
  )

> (when-ex2 5)

> (when-ex2 39)

> (when-ex2 11)
```

What is the value of each of the following expressions?

(when t (+ 1 2) (+ 3 4))

(when nil (+ 1 2) (+ 3 4))

(setf x '(a b c))

(when (listp x) (princ (car x)) (terpri) (cdr x))

(when (numberp x) (princ x) (terpri) (− x 1))

Describe how **when** works. What value does it return?

There are two main differences between **when** and **if**. What are they?

Write a function of one argument which should be a positive integer. The function is to print the argument and the positive integers less than it, one per line. Use **when**. The value the function returns may be **nil**.

A Lisp function (technically a macro) which is similar to **when** is **unless**. Find out how **unless** works by entering expresssions. Here are two to start.
(unless t (princ "YES") (terpri))
(unless nil (princ "AHA") (terpri))

Describe how **unless** works.

SUMMARY

Eql is a predicate which tests whether expressions are the same (in some sense). (There are other equality predicates.) **Atom** and **stringp** are predicates which test the type of their arguments. **Zerop** tests for the value **0**.

Princ causes a value to be printed. **Terpri** starts a new line.

Format returns a string constructed from its arguments to an output device. When the first argument of **format** is **nil**, output is sent to the default output device. ~A denotes places in the format string where the ASCII string corresponding to an argument is to appear.

Not, **or** and **and** are logical functions. When using these, any value which is not **nil** is (roughly speaking) considered to have the value true.

If, **when** and **unless** cause an expression or expressions to be evaluated depending on whether an expression is **nil** or not.

LESSON 5
List Manipulation (2)

Enter the following.

> (setf s 'a-symbol)

> (setf l '(a b c d))

> (cons s l)

> (list s l)

> (append s l)

> (cons l l)

> (list l l)

> (append l l)

> (append '(1 2 3) l)

> (append l '(1 2 3))

> (list s s)

> (list s s s s s)

> (list 1 2 3 4 5)

> (list l l l)

> (cons s ())

> (append () ())

> (list () ())

> (cons () ())

> (cons () l)

> (append () l)

> (list () l)

> (list l (list l l))

> (list (+ 1 2) (listp l) s)

What values are returned by the following?

(cons 'a '(x y z))

(list 'a '(x y z))

(cons '(a) '(x y z))

(append '(a) '(x y z))

(list '(a) '(x y z))

(cons '(x y z) ())

(append '(x y z) ())

(list '(x y z) ())

(list 'a 'x 'y 'z)

Write an expression which uses the lists **(1 2 3)**, **(4 5 6)** and **(7 8 9)** to make one list consisting of the numbers from **1** to **9**.

LESSON 5

Write an expression which uses the lists **(1 2 3)**, **(4 5 6)** and **(7 8 9)** to make a list consisting of these three lists.

cons, **list** and **append** are all used to construct lists. Describe what they do and how they differ.

Write a function which works something like **cons** in that a list and an object are used to form one list. However, the function you write is to add the object at the end of the list (instead of the beginning which is what **cons** does). For example, if the function is named **snoc** (**cons** in reverse)
(snoc '(a b c) 'd) => **'(a b c d)**

Enter the following.

> (setf l '(a b c d e))

> (first l)

> (second l)

> (third l)

> (fourth l)

> (fifth l)

> (sixth l)

> (seventh l)

> (setf ll (append l '(u v w x y z)))

> (sixth ll)

> (seventh ll)

> (eighth ll)

> (ninth ll)

> (tenth ll)

> (eleventh ll)

> (setf l '((a b c) (1 2 3) (x y z)))

> (first l)

> (first (first l))

> (first (second l))

> (second (first l))

> (third (third l))

What are the values of the following expressions?

(second '((1 2) (2 3) (3 4) (4 5)))

(second (third '((1 2) (3 4 5) (6 7 8) (9 10 11))))

(third (second '((1 2) (3 4 5) (6 7 8) (9 10 11))))

Use **first**, **second**, **third**, and so forth applied to the list **((1 2 3 4) 6 7 (8 9 10 11))** to return each of the values **2**, **4**, **6**, **8**.

LESSON 5

Write a function which has one argument which is a list. The function is to return a list of four lists. The first list within the list consists of the symbols in the argument list. The second list with the list returned contains the numbers in the argument list. The third list within the list consists of lists in the original list. The last list within the list consists of everything else in the original list. If, for example, there are no symbols in the argument list, the first list within the list returned should be **nil**. For example, (naming the function **organize**)

(organize '(a b c 4 (x y z) d 5 "help"
      e '(u v w) f g
)
) =>
((A B C D E F G) (4 5) ((X Y Z) (U V W)) ("help"))
(organize '(x y (a b) (c d) "JUNK" z "YARD")) =>
((X Y Z) NIL ((A B) (C D)) ("JUNK" "YARD"))

The **nil** in the second example signifies that there were no numbers in the original list. It may be helpful to write functions which add an item to a list of lists in a specified place. For example, **put-second** could be defined to add an item to the second list of a list.
(put-second 'x '((a b) (c d) (e f) (g h))) =>
    ((a b) (x c d) (e f) (g h))

Hint: What is returned when the list is empty?

Enter the following.

> (setf l '(a b c d))

> (reverse l)

> (reverse "Hello")

> (reverse (reverse l))

> (eq l (reverse (reverse l)))

> (eql l (reverse (reverse l)))

> (equal l (reverse (reverse l)))

> (setf s "This is a string.")

> (reverse s)

> (reverse (reverse s))

> (eq s (reverse (reverse s)))

> (eql s (reverse (reverse s)))

> (equal s (reverse (reverse s)))

> (setf ll '((a b c) (d e f) (g h i)))

> (reverse ll)

> (reverse (car (reverse ll)))

> (length l)

> (length s)

> (length ll)

> (length (reverse l))

> (eq (length l) (length (reverse l)))

> (length "Hello there")

What are the values of the following?

(reverse '(1 2 3))

(reverse "Lisp is fun.")

(reverse '((1 2) (3 4) (5 6)))

LESSON 5

(setf l '(a b c d))

(reverse (cons (car l) (reverse (cdr l))))

(length ())

(length '(a b c d e f g))

(length '(a b (c d) e (f g)))

(length "Lisp is fun.")

Write a function which tests if a string is a palindrome (reads the same forward and backwards (e.g., "POP"). The function should return **nil**, if its argument is not a string or is a string which is not a palindrome. Otherwise, it should return a non-**nil** value.

The function **length** for lists (only) can be written using **cond** (or **if**), **null**, **t** and some simple arithmetic. Define **len**, a function which returns the number of objects in a list using **cond**, etc. Do not count the items within sublists. For example,
(len '(a b (d e f g))) => 3

The function **reverse** is also easy to write for lists. Write a function which returns the reverse of a list. For example,
(rev '(a b c (d e f)) x) => (x (d e f) c b a)

Note that lists within the list are not reversed.

Enter the following.

> (max 3 4)

> (max 3 4 5 6)

> (max 6 5 4 3)

> (max 1 6 2 2)

> (max 3 3 3)

> (max 88)

What does **max** do?

Write a function which returns the length of the largest list within a list. Note: the length of the longest string should not be returned. For example, if the function is named **longest-list-len** then
(longest-list-len '((a b) x 9 (c d e) "Hello"))
  => **3**

Explore and discover what **min** returns. (It is analogous to **max**.)

Enter the following.

> (setf L '(a b c d))

> L

> (setf (car L) 'aa)

> L

LESSON 5

> (setq (car L) 'aaa)

> L

> (setf (car L) '(x y))

> L

> (setf (car L) 'a)

> L

> (setf LL '(a b c d))

> LL

> (eql L LL)

> (setf LL L)

> LL

> (eql L LL)

> (setf (car L) 'x)

> L

> LL

> (eql L LL)

> (setf L (cons 'a (cdr L)))

> L

> LL

> (eql L LL)

> (setf LL L)

> L

> LL

> (eql L LL)

> (rplaca L 'z)   ; RePLAce CAr

> L

> LL

> (eql L LL)

> (rplaca LL 'a)

> L

> LL

> (eql L LL)

> (setf s 'a-symbol)

> s

> (setf (car s) 'another-symbol)

> s

> (rplaca s 'yet-another-symbol)

> s

What is the value of **L** after each of the following expressions are evaluated?

(setf L '(alpha beta gamma))

(setf L LL)

(setf (car LL) 'aleph)

(rplaca L 'alif)

Can **setq** be used wherever **setf** can be used? If not, give an example of where **setf** can be used but **setq** can't.

If **L** is a list is there any difference between the effect (on L) of **(rplaca L 'a)** and **(setf (car L) 'a)**?

If **L** is a list, what is the difference between the values returned by **(rplaca L 'a)** and **(setf (car L) 'a)**?

If **L** is a list is there any difference between the effect of **(setf (car L) 'a))** and **(setf L (cons 'a (cdr L)))**? If there is a difference, what is it?

Suppose **L** and **LL** are both lists and that
L => (A B C)
LL => (A B C)

Does this guarantee **(eql L LL)** is not **nil**?

Enter the following.

> (setf L '(a b c))

> (setf (cdr L) '(d e f))

> L

> (setq (cdr L) '(x y z))

> L

> (setf LL L)

> LL

> (eql L LL)

> (setf (cdr L) '(1 2 3))

> L

> LL

> (eql L LL)

> (setf L '(a b c d))

> (setf LL L)

> (rplacd L '(x y z))   ; RePLAce CDr

> L

> LL

> (eql L LL)

    What is the value of L after each of the following expresssions is evaluated?

    (setf L '(one two three))

    (setf LL L)

    (setf (cdr LL) '(deux trois))

    (rplacd L '(dos tres))

    If L is a list, is there any difference in the effect (upon L) between **(setf (cdr L) '(a b c))** and **(rplacd L '(a b c))**?

    If L is a list, what is the difference between the values returned by **(setf (cdr L) '(a b c))** and **(rplacd L '(a b c))**?

LESSON 5

Suppose **L** and **LL** are lists and suppose the following expresssions are evaluated.

(setf (car L) (car LL))

(setf (cdr L) (cdr LL))

Will **(eql L LL)** be **nonnil** ?

Enter the following.

> (setf L '(a b c d e))

> L

> (setf (first L) 1)

> L

> (setf (second L) 2)

> L

> (setf (rest L) '(20 30 40))

> L

> (setf (cadr L) 200)

> L

> (setf (caddr L) 300)

> L

> (setf (cddr L) '(p q r s))

> L

> (setf (cdddr L) '(x y z))

> L

What is the value of **L** after each of the following expressions is evaluated?

(setf L '(a b c d e f))

(setf (first L) 'aa)

(setf (rest L) '(bb cc dd ee ff))

(setf (cadr L) 'x)

(setf (cddr L) '(u v w))

Suppose the value of **L** is the list **(1 2 3 4 5)**. Give two expressions which (when evaluated) will have the effect of replacing the **2** in the list so that **L** will have the value **(1 20 3 4 5)**. The expressions should only refer to **L** and **20**. (That is, cheap shots: **(setf L '(1 20 3 4 5))** are not permitted.)

SUMMARY

List and **append** are Lisp functions which build lists.

The functions **third**, **fourth**, ... **tenth** return elements of a list.

Reverse returns a list or string in reverse order. The function **length** returns the number of objects (characters) in a list (string).

Eq and **equal** are Lisp predicates which test whether two objects are the same (in some sense). **Eq** is the more stringent (i.e. will return **nil** more often) and **equal** is the less stringent. **Eql** falls between **eq** and **equal**.

Max and **min** are functions for determining the largest and smallest elements in a list of numbers.

Setf can be used to alter part of a list. **Rplaca** and **rplacd** are used to replace the **car** and **cdr** of a list.

LESSON 6
The Common LISP Programming Environment

;; ** Although all the functions utilized in this
;; ** lesson are Common Lisp, most of them are (to
;; ** a greater or lesser extent) implementation
;; ** dependent.

Enter the following.

> (lisp-implementation-type)

> (lisp-implementation-version)

> (machine-type)

> (machine-version)

> (machine-instance)

> (software-type)

> (software-version)

> (short-site-name)

> (long-site-name)

> internal-time-units-per-second   ; No parentheses

Using the values returned above, answer the following (if possible). Note when a question cannot be answered using the above.

What is the name of implementation of the Common Lisp you Lisp you use?

Which version (number) is the implementation of the Common the Common Lisp you use?

What is the name of the computer on which you are running running Common Lisp?

What other software (e.g. operating system) is the Common the Common Lisp you use dependent upon?

How useful do you think the information returned above is?

Enter the following.

> (get-decoded-time)

Compare the second and third values returned above with the time (minutes and hours) of day. (Hours go from 1 to 24.)

Compare the fourth, fifth and sixth values returned above with the date. (January is considered month 0.)

If there doesn't seem to be some connection in the preceding, check (or have the responsible person check) the date and time setting on the system.

Compare the seventh value returned with the day of the week considering Monday as day 0.

Enter the following. (Of course, it is not necessary to enter the comments.)

```
> (dribble "<file-name>")        ;; **  <file-name> must conform to the
                                 ;; **  file naming conventions of the
                                 ;; **  system.

> (room)

> (defun fib(n)                  ; Nth Fibonacci number,
        (cond                    ; just for an example.
            ((zerop n) 1)
            ((= n 1)      1)
            (t (+ (fib (− n 1)) (fib (− n 2))))
        )
  )
```

LESSON 6

> (room)

> (fib 0)   ; test

> (fib 1)   ; test

> (fib 3)   ; test

> (fib 6)   ; test

> (dribble)

What effect did defining **fib** have upon the memory being used by the Lisp system?

Leave the Common Lisp system and examine the file named in the first use of **dribble**. (E.g. in MS-DOS use the type command, in UNIX, use the cat command.)

Using whatever text editor is convenient, edit the file so that it includes just the definition of **fib**. This means deleting everything that's not in the list which begins with **defun**.

Start the Lisp system and then enter the following.

> (fib 5)

> (load "<file-name>")   ; <file-name> is the name of the file just edited.

> (fib 5)

Exit the Lisp system and use an editor to create a file which has the following contents.
(defun sq(x) (* x x))

Start the Lisp system and then enter the following.

> (sq 7)

> (load "<sq-file>")   ; <sq-file> is the name of the file just created.

> (sq 7)

How is **load** useful?

Enter the following. If the definition of **fib** is still in a file, use **(load "<file-name>")** instead of **defun**.

```
> (defun fib(n)                              ; Nth Fibonacci number, just for an example.
        (cond
              ((zerop n) 1)
              ((= n 1)      1)
              (t (+ (fib (− n 1)) (fib (− n 2))))
        )
  )

> (describe 'fib)

> (setf L '(a b c))

> (describe 'L)

> (inspect 'fib)                             ;; ** Exactly what inspect will do
                                             ;; ** is (by definition) implementation-dependent.
                                             ;; ** However, a
                                             ;; ** good bet is that a prompt will
                                             ;; ** appear. Try entering H or ?
                                             ;; ** to get help. It should be
                                             ;; ** possible to access and modify
                                             ;; ** parts associated with the
                                             ;; ** symbol. Spend some time
                                             ;; ** trying the options provided
                                             ;; ** by inspect.
```

What values or definitions associated with a symbol (e.g., a function) are returned by **describe**?

What happens when **inspect** is used? What commands does **inspect** provide? How is help obtained (if at all) in **inspect**?

Enter the following. (**Fib** is still the Fibonacci function.) Note the times that are reported.

```
> (time (fib 5))

> (time (fib 10))

> (time (fib 15))

> (time (fib 20))

> (time (fib 25))

> (time (fib 30))

> (describe 'fib)
```

LESSON 6

> (room)

> (compile 'fib)

> (describe 'fib)

> (room)

> (time (fib 5))

> (time (fib 10))

> (time (fib 15))

> (time (fib 20))

> (time (fib 25))

> (time (fib 30))

> (defun naptime(n)
>   (sleep n)
>   (format nil "Time to wake up.")
>)

> (naptime 20)

> (naptime 40)

> (time (sleep 20))

> (time (sleep 40))

What information does **time** return?

What is the purpose of **sleep**? What does its argument (a number) denote?

What does **compile** do? Compare the times of **fib** before and after compilation. Compare the description of **fib** given by **describe** before and after compilation. Is the original definition of **fib** (i.e. the one made with **defun**) available after compilation? Does compiling save space?

Enter the following.

> (defun sq(x) (* x x))

> (sq 4)   ; Test

```
>   (step (sq 4))                         ;; **    Step is implementation dependent.
                                          ;; **    Probably a prompt will
                                          ;; **    be printed. Enter a ? or h to
                                          ;; **    obtain help. Use some of the
                                          ;; **    options available and see what
                                          ;; **    they do.

>   (compile 'sq)

>   (step (sq 4))

>   (defun symlist(L)                     ; A recursive example.
        (cond
            ((null L) ())
            ((symbolp (car L))
                (cons (car L) (symlist (cdr L)))
            )
            (t (symlist (cdr L)))
        )
    )

>   (symlist '(a b c 1 2 3 (x y z) d e f))   ; Test

>   (step (symlist '(a 1 (x y) b))
```

What options does **step** (in your implementation) provide? Describe how they are used.

Compare how **step** works with compiled functions and interpreted functions. In terms of debugging which is more useful?

Earlier the function **trace** was introduced for "watching" a function. Compare **step** and **trace** as debugging aids. What are their advantages and disadvantages?

SUMMARY

A number of functions provide information about the system: **lisp-implementation-type**, **lisp-implementation-version**, **machine-type**, **machine-version**, **machine-instance**, **software-type**, **software-version**, **short-site-name**, and **long-site-name**

The constant **internal-time-units-per-second** gives information about the machine cycle. The function **get-decoded-time** provides the date and time.

Dribble puts a transcript of a Lisp session in a file. **Load** reads a file into the Lisp environment.

Step allows the programmer to "watch" a function's execution. **Describe** and **inspect** give system information about a function. **Inspect** allows the programmer to alter a function's definition.

Room gives information about memory. **Time** times a function's execution.

Compile compiles a function (changes the function's **d**escription to machine code).

Sleep is used for pauses.

LESSON 7
Output and Strings

Enter the following. (Much of this lesson doesn't use any new Lisp constructs.)

> (setf a-symbol 'whatever)

> (princ a-symbol)

> (symbolp (princ a-symbol))

> (setf x 10)

> (princ x)

> (numberp (princ x))

> (+ (princ x) (princ x))

> (setf a-list '(a b c))

> (princ a-list)

> (listp (princ a-list))

> (null (princ a-list))

LESSON 7

> (car (princ a-list))

> (stringp "hello")

> (stringp 'a)

> (stringp 1000)

> (setf greeting "hello")

> (stringp greeting)

> (princ greeting)

> (stringp (princ greeting))

> (format nil "Hello there")

> (princ (format nil "Hello there"))

> (stringp (format nil "Hello there"))

> (stringp (princ (format nil "Hello there")))

> (setf greeting "Hello there")

> greeting

> (princ (format nil "~a" greeting))

> (princ (format nil "~a ~a" greeting greeting))

> (stringp (princ
        (format nil "~a ~a" greeting greeting)
)
)

> (setf another-greeting "How are you today?")

> (princ (format nil "~a ~a" greeting another-greeting))

> (format nil "~a ~a ~a"
    greeting another-greeting greeting
)

> (format nil "~a ~a" greeting)

> (format nil "~a" greeting another-greeting)

> (princ (format nil "~a + ~a = ~a" 2 3 5))

> (princ (format nil "~a + ~a = ~a" 2 3 (+ 2 3)))

> (defun greet (n)
       (princ (format nil "Hello, ~a" n))
)

> (greet "George")

> (greet 'george)

> (greet '(a b c))

What does **princ** do? What value does it return? What is the type of the value returned by **princ**?

What is the purpose of ~**a** in the string (called the control-string) of a **format** function?

Write a function of two arguments (both numbers) which outputs their sum as an arithmetic addition. For example,
(adder 9 8) => 9 + 8 = 17

Enter the following.

LESSON 7

```
>   (setf n 99)

>   (let (n)                               ; n is called a local variable.
        (setf n 10)
        (princ n)
        (princ " ")
        (princ (+ n n))
        (princ " ")
        (princ (* n n))
    )

>   n

>   (let ()
        (setf n 10)
        (princ n)
        (princ " ")
        (princ (+ n n))
        (princ " ")
        (princ (* n n))
    )

>   n

>   (setf m 100)

>   (let (m n)
        (setf m 8)
        (setf n 88)
        (princ (+ m n))
        (princ " ")
        (princ (* m n))
    )

>   m

>   n

>   (null (let (a) (setf a 'a-symbol) (princ a)))

>   (null (let () ))                       ; Of course this is a little silly.
```

What is returned when the following expressions are entered? Assume they are entered without interruption.

(setf x 10)

(setf xx 20)

```
(let (x xx)
  (setf x 100)
  (setf xx 1000)
  (princ (+ x xx))
)
```

x

xx

```
(let ()
  (setf x 100)
  (setf xx 1000)
  (princ (+ x xx))
)
```

x

xx

Explain how the results in the above occurred. In particular, explain the values of **x** and **xx** that are returned.

What is the purpose of **let**? A list (possibly **nil**) follows **let**. What is its purpose?

Enter the following.

> (setf m 888 n 999)

LESSON 7

> m

> n

> (let ((m 10) (n 20))
    (princ m)
    (princ " ")
    (princ n)
)

> m

> n

> (defun greeter(name)
    (let ((blank " "))
       (princ "Hello,")
       (princ blank)
       (princ name)
       (princ blank)
       (princ "How are you?")
)
)

> (greeter "George")

> (greeter 'george)

What is printed when the following is entered?

(let ((u "UP") (d "DOWN"))
  (princ u)
  (princ " and ")
  (princ d)
)

Redefine the function **greeter** so that it does the same thing but only uses three **princ**s and does not need the variable **blank**.

Redefine the function **greeter** so that it does the same thing but only uses one **princ**, a **format** and does not need the variable blank.

What is the effect of the list **(ix 9)** occurring in the list following a **let**?

What is the purpose of putting a two element list in the list which follows a **let**?

Enter the following.

> (let (a b)
      (princ a)
      (princ b)
)

> (let ((a 'a-value) b)
      (princ a)
      (princ b)
)

> (let (a (b 'another-value))
      (princ a)
      (princ b)
)

> (boundp 'xxx)

> (setq xxx '(x y z))

> (boundp 'xxx)

LESSON 7

> (boundp 'yyy)

> (let (yyy)
        (princ (boundp yyy))
)

> (boundp 'yyy)

What is the value of a local variable of a **let** if none is supplied?

What is output when the following is entered?

(let (x (y 'junk))
  (princ (cons y x))
)

What is the purpose of **boundp**?

Are the local variables of a **let** always bound?

Enter the following.

> (let ()
        (princ 'a)
        (princ 'b)
        (princ 'c)
)

> (let ()
        (princ 'a)
        (terpri)
        (princ 'b)
        (terpri)
        (princ 'c)
)

> (let()
      (princ 'a)
      (terpri)
      (terpri)
      (princ 'b)
      (terpri)
      (terpri)
      (terpri)
      (princ 'c)
)

> (terpri)

> (null (terpri))

What value does **terpri** return?

Enter the following.

> (setf greeting "Hello")

> (setf another-greeting "Good morning")

> (format nil "~a ~%~a" greeting another-greeting)

> (princ
     (format nil "~a~%~a" greeting another-greeting)
)

> (princ
     (format nil "~a~%~%~a" greeting another-greeting)
)

> (princ
     (format nil "~a~5%~a" greeting another-greeting)
)

What is the purpose of ~% in the control-string of the **format** function?

LESSON 7

What does ~8% cause when it occurs in a control-string of a **format** function?

```
;; ** In the next two examples the tilde (~) at the end
;; ** of a line is followed immediately by <RET> (the
;; ** return or enter key).
> ( format    nil       "The spaces at the beginning don't~
leave room for the rest."
       )
> (format nil "This ~
          is ~
          a ~
          silly ~
          way ~
          to ~
          enter ~
          a ~
          string."
  )
```

What happens when a tilde (~) is followed immediately by a <RET> in the control-string of a **format** function?

Enter the following.

```
> (snoc 'x '(a b c))

> (defun add-both-ends (x L)
     (labels ( (snoc(x L)              ; snoc is cons backwards.
                  (cond
                     ((null L) (list x))
                     (t (cons (car L) (snoc x (cdr L))))
                )
```

```
                              )
                          )
                  (cons x (snoc x L))
              )
          )

>   (add-both-ends 'a '(1 2 3))

>   (snoc 'x '(a b c))

>   (defun medalists (field)
        (labels ( (runners-up (L1) (rest L1))
                  (gold (L2) (first L2))
                  (silver (L3) (gold (runners-up L3)))
                  (bronze (L4) (silver (runners-up L4)))
                )
            (princ
                (format nil "Gold medalist : ~a~%" (gold field))
            )
            (princ
                (format nil "Silver medalist : ~a~% (silver field))
            )
            (princ
                (format nil "Bronze medalist : ~a~%" (bronze field))
            )
        )
    )

>   (setf f '(jones smith green white))

>   (medalists f)

>   (runnersup f)

>   (gold f)

>   (medalists (cons 'brown f))

>   (> 2 3)                        ; These four are in preparation for
                                   ; the next function's definition.

>   (> 3 2)

>   (> 2 3 4 5)

>   (> 2 3 4 1)
```

LESSON 7

```
>   (defun bordered-blanks (n)
        (let ( (blank #\Space) (mark #\*) )
           (labels ((print-blanks (n)
                               (when (> n 0) (princ blank) (print-blanks (- n 1)))
                       )
                   )
               (princ mark)
               (print-blanks (- n 2))
               (princ mark)
               (terpri)
           )
        )
    )

>   (bordered-blanks 8)

>   (bordered-blanks 2)

>   (bordered-blanks 0)

>   blank

>   mark

>   (print-blanks 7)

>   (defun bordered-blanks2 (n)
       (labels ( (print-blanks (b n)
                               (when (> n 0)
                                   (princ b)
                                   (print-blanks b (- n 1))
                               )
                     )
                 )
           (let ( (blank #\Space) (mark #\*) )
               (princ mark)
               (print-blanks blank (- n 2))
               (princ mark)
               (terpri)
           )
        )
    )

>   (bordered-blanks2 8)

>   (bordered-blanks2 2)

>   (bordered-blanks2 0)
```

Immediately following **labels** there is a list (of lists). What is in the list? Compare with the objects that follow **defun** in a function definition.

Are the functions that are defined using **labels** accessible outside **labels**?

Write a function which returns a list with both the first and last element of the list removed. If the function is named **cdrrdc** then
(cdrrdc '(a b c d e f)) => (B C D E)

Use **labels** to define a function within **cdrrdc** which returns a list with the last element removed. [Hint: use **reverse**.]

Describe how < works.

Consider the following version of bordered-blanks.

```
(defun bordered-blanks3 (n)
  (labels ( (print-blanks (n)
              (when (> n 0)
                (princ blank)
                (print-blanks (- n 1)))
            )
          )
    (let ( (blank #\Space) (mark #\*) )
      (princ mark)
```

```
      (print-blanks (− n 2))
      (princ mark)
      (terpri)
    )
  )
)
```

Bordered-blanks3 probably won't work. Why? Why don't we say it certainly won't work?

SUMMARY

Let and **labels** are used to "localize" an effect. **Let** is used for local variables. **Labels** is used for local functions.

New lines within the control string of a **format** function can be controlled with ~% (or even ~n%, n a number) and ~<**RET**>. The first causes a new line to be started. The second allows the control string to extend over more than one line.

Boundp is a predicate which returns whether a symbol currently has a value.

LESSON 8

The Read, Evaluate, and Output Loop

;; ** The format of this lesson differs somewhat from
;; ** that of previous lessons.

The usual notation for arithmetic and algebraic expressions is infix notation. That is, the operator (+ − * /) occurs between the operands (numbers, variables or expressions) for the operator. In contrast, Lisp uses prefix notation; the operator occurs before the operands.

Write a (Lisp) function which converts an infix expression into a prefix (Lisp) expression. Assume that the operators in the infix expression are explicit. For example, 3b is not used, (3 * b) is. Also assume that the infix expression is completely parenthesized. For example, (3 + a) not 3 + a and ((3 * x) + 7) not 3 * x + 7 . Name the function **prefix**. Here are some instances of **prefix**.

>   **(prefix '(8 + 9)) => (+ 8 9)**

>   **(prefix '(8 + (3 * 4))) => (+ 8 (* 3 4))**

>   **(prefix '((x + y) * (3 + z)))**
>   **=> (* (+ X Y) (+ 3 Z))**

>   **(prefix 8) => 8**

>   **(prefix 'x) => X**

    Here are the specifics. The legal arguments for **prefix** are numbers, symbols and expressions of the form (**infix-expr-1 operator infix-expr-2**) where **operator** is an

LESSON 8

arithmetic operator and **infix-expr-1** and **infix-expr-2** are also expressions. (The parentheses must be present.)

If **number** is a number (e.g., **9, 22.5**) then

(prefix number) => number

If **symbol** is a symbol (e.g., **'x, 'whatever**) then

(prefix symbol) => symbol

If an (infix) expression is given (it must be quoted) then

(prefix '(in-expr1 operator in-expr2)) =>

(operator (prefix in-expr1) (prefix in-expr2))

If the argument is to the function is not one of these, the function just returns the symbol ERROR.

This is not as hard as one might suppose. Just use the description above as the basis for the function **prefix**.

Save **prefix** for later use. One way to do this is to create a file holding the definition of **prefix** (and any functions **prefix** calls) and load it into Lisp using **(load "file-name")** where file-name is the name of the file in which prefix is stored. Enter the following.

> '(+ 3 4)

> (eval '(+ 3 4))

> (listp '(+ 3 4))

> (listp (eval '(+ 3 4)))

> '(car '(a b c))

> (eval '(car '(a b c)))

> (setf L '(a b c))

> '(car L)

> (eval '(car L))

> (setf seven '(+ 3 4))

> seven

> (listp seven)

> (eval seven)

> (1+ (eval seven))

> (setf xx 20)

> 'xx

> xx

> (eval xx)

> (eval 'xx)

> (eval '(* xx xx))

> '(* xx xx)

> (setf forty '(* 2 xx))

> forty

> (eval forty)

What are the values of the following expressions? (Assume they are entered without interruption.)

(setf a-product '(* 3 4 5))

a-product

(listp a-product)

(numberp a-product)

(eval a-product)

(listp (eval a-product))

(numberp (eval a-product))

Give an expression in which **eval** is applied to an argument and returns a list.

LESSON 8

What is the purpose of the function **eval**?

Using the function **prefix** that was written earlier, write an infix expression evaluator. (The infix expressions must be given in the form prescribed for **prefix**.) This is very easy. For example, suppose the function is named in-val, then

(in-val '(3 + 4)) => 7

(in-val '((3 + 4) * (9 − 8))) => 7

(setf x 10)   ; Just to give x a value for the next example.

(in-val '(x * (x + 9))) => 190

Save this function for later use.

Enter the following.

> (type-of 9)

> (type-of 12345678900)

> (type-of 'x)

> (type-of x)

> (setf x 10)

> (type-of x)

> (type-of '(a b c))

> (type-of (+ 4 6))

> (type-of 7/8)

> (type-of 8/8)

> (type-of 9.3)

What is the purpose of the function **type-of**?

Enter the following. When **read** is evaluated, Lisp waits for input. Thus there may be two expressions after one prompt. The second expression (which may be a number or symbol) is to be entered as input to the first expression. For example, after **(setq eight (read))** of the first prompt below, **8** is to be entered.

```
>   (setq eight (read))
8

>   eight

>   (* 2 (read))
12

>   (car (read))
(a b c)

>   (defun typer () (type-of (read)))

>   (typer)
9

>   (typer)
x

>   (typer)
(a b c)

>   (typer)
"HELLO"

>   (defun reader ()
        (princ "*—>")
        (setf x (read))
        (princ (format nil "— ~a —~%" x))
        (if (not (eq x 'quit)) (reader))
    )
```
;; ** When **reader** is evaluated a new prompt (*—>)
;; ** will appear. Expressions for this prompt are
;; ** given where they are needed. Enter the
;; ** following.

```
>   (setf twenty 20)
```

LESSON 8   91

> (reader)

*—>   9

*—>   (a b c)

*—>   x

*—>   "HELLO"

*—>   "This is a little longer and extends over
         two lines"

*—>   twenty

*—>   (setf thirty 30)

*—>   quit   ; This should stop reader and return the Lisp prompt.

> thirty

What does the function **read** do? When an expression is read by **read** is it evaluated?

Using the functions written earlier (**prefix** and **in-val**) write a function which evaluates "regular" expressions (i.e. infix expressions as described at the beginning of this lesson). The function is to repeatedly issue a prompt and then return the value of the parenthesized infix expression that is entered. The function should stop when the number **0** is entered. For example, (assuming the function is named **evaluate** and it issues the prompt ****>**):

> (evaluate)
**> (3 + 4)
= 7
**> (9 − 9)
= 0
**> ((4 + 6) * (9 − 4))
= 50

```
**> 0
>
```

Enter the following. Note that within the functions **eval-fun** and **princ-fun** the same expression **(cons fun L)** occurs. Contrast **eval**'s and **princ**'s use of this expression.

> (defun eval-fun (fun L) (eval (cons fun L)))

> (defun princ-fun (fun L)
     (princ (cons fun L))
     (terpri)
)

> (eval-fun '+ '(2 3 4))

> (princ-fun '+ '(2 3 4))

> (eval-fun 'list '(2 3 4))

> (princ-fun 'list '(2 3 4))

> (eval-fun 'list '(a b c))

> (princ-fun 'list '(a b c))

> (setq a 'a b 'b c 'c)

> (eval-fun 'list '(a b c))

> (princ-fun 'list '(a b c))

> (eval-fun '+ '(2 3 x))

> (princ-fun '+ '(2 3 x))

> (setq x 10)

> (eval-fun '+ '(2 3 x))

> (princ-fun '+ '(2 3 x))

> (setq plus '+)

> (plus 2 3 4)

LESSON 8

> (eval-fun plus '(2 3 4))

> (princ-fun plus '(2 3 4))

> (setq L '(2 3 4))

> (eval-fun '+ L)

> (princ-fun '+ L)

> (eval-fun 'list L)

> (princ-fun 'list L)

> (eval-fun plus L)

> (princ-fun plus L)

> (eval-fun 'car '('(x y z)))

> (princ-fun 'car '('(x y z)))

When a quoted expression is given to a function as a parameter (e.g., '+ or '(2 3 4) in the preceding), what happens to the quote (roughly speaking)?

Suppose **princ-simp** is defined as follows.

defun princ-simp (x) (princ x) (terpri))

What would be *printed* by the following?

(princ-simp 'x)

(princ-simp ''x)

(princ-simp '(a b c))

(princ-simp ''(a b c))

When **eval** is applied to a quoted expression (e.g. **(eval '(+ 2 3)))** what happens to the quote (roughly speaking)?

Suppose **eval-simp** is defined as follows.

(defun eval-simp (x) (eval x))

What are the values (if any) of the following?

(eval-simp 'a)

(eval-simp "a)

(eval-simp '(a b c))

(eval-simp "(a b c))

SUMMARY

Eval evaluates a (correctly formed) Lisp expression.

Read returns an expression read from the default input. (The expression is not evaluated.)

Type-of returns the type of an expression.

LESSON 9
Parameter Passing

Enter the following.

> (defun par-ex1 (x y &optional z)
        (princ (format nil "~a ~a ~a" x y z))
        (terpri)
)

> (par-ex1 1 2)

> (par-ex1 1 2 3)

> (par-ex1 'a 'b)

> (par-ex1 'a 'b 'c)

> (par-ex1 '(a b) '(c d))

> (par-ex1 '(a b) '(c d) '(e f))

> (defun par-ex2 (x &optional y z)
       (princ (format nil "~a ~a ~a" x y z))
       (terpri)
)

> (par-ex2 1)

> (par-ex2 1 2)

> (par-ex2 1 2 3)

> (par-ex2 'a 'b)

> (par-ex2 'a 'b 'c)

> (par-ex2 (+ 2 3))

> (defun par-ex3 (&optional x y)
      (cond
          ((null x) (princ "No values entered"))
          (t (princ (format nil "~a ~a" x y)))
)
      (terpri)
)

> (par-ex3)

> (par-ex3 8)

> (par-ex3 8 9)

Suppose **par-q1** is defined as follows.

(defun par-q1 (a b &optional c d)
   (princ (format nil "~a ~a ~a ~a" a b c d))
   (terpri)
)

What is output by the following uses of **par-q1**?

(par-q1 1 2)

(par-q1 1 2 3)

(par-q1 1 2 3 4)

(par-q1 3 2 1)

What is the purpose of **&optional** in a parameter list?

LESSON 9

Can more than one parameter follow **&optional**?

What is the value of an **&optional** parameter if none is supplied when the function is evaluated?

Enter the following.

> (defun par-ex4 (x &optional (xx 20))
>   (princ (format nil "~a ~a" x xx))
>   (terpri)
>)

> (par-ex4 5 6)

> (par-ex4 0)

> (par-ex4 2 3)

> (par-ex4 7)

> (par-ex4 'a)

> (par-ex4 'a 'b)

> (par-ex4 '(a b c))

> (par-ex4 '(a b c) '(d e f))

> (defun par-ex5 (&optional (x 10) (xx 20))
>   (princ (format nil "~a ~a" x xx))
>   (terpri)
>)

> (par-ex5 1 2)

> (par-ex5 2)

> (par-ex5)

> (par-ex5 3 4 5)

> (par-ex5 'a)

> (par-ex5 '(a b c))

Suppose the function **par-q2** is defined as follows.

```
(defun par-q2 (&optional (a 11) (b 12))
  (princ (format nil "~a ~a" a b))
  (terpri)
)
```

What is output by the following?

(par-q2)

(par-q2 99)

(par-q2 10 20)

(par-q2 (+ 5 6))

If **(xxx 30)** follows **&optional** in a parameter list what is the default value of **xxx**?

Write a function which returns the sum of up to four values (which should be numbers). If one (or more) of the values is not a number, it should not be used in computing the sum. For example, if the function is named **add-em**,

(add-em 2 3) => 5

(add-em 2 3 'x) => 5

(add-em) => 0

In a number of the example functions, the construct

(princ (format nil "CONTROL STRING" arguments)) (terpri)

LESSON 9

has been used to produce reasonable looking output. (We have used **terpri** instead of ~% in the control string to avoid having the value of the **princ** expression returned.) Write a function, **s-print** (for simple print), which embodies this construct. The first parameter of **s-print** is a string which is used as the control string for formatting. The remaining parameters (up to five) are all optional and give values to be printed. For example,

(s-print "~a + ~a = ~a" 2 3 5)

would cause

2 + 3 = 5

to be printed and

(s-print "First: ~a ~% Rest: ~a" (car '(x y z)) (cdr '(x y z)))

would cause

First: X Rest: (Y Z)

to be printed. The function should always cause a new line after printing. If this function is saved, it may be used in the exercises that follow (in place of **princ**, and so on) and make things a little simpler.

Enter the following.

> (defun par-ex6 (x &rest y)
>   (princ (format nil "~a ~a" x y))
>   (terpri)
>)

> (par-ex6 8)

> (par-ex6 8 9)

> (par-ex6 4 5 6)

> (par-ex6 4 5 6 7)

> (par-ex6 3 4 5 6 7 8)

> (par-ex6 '(1 2 3))

> (par-ex6 'a)

> (par-ex6 'a 'b)

> (par-ex6 '(a b))

> (par-ex6 '(a b c) '(d e f))

> (defun par-ex7 (x y &rest z)
        (princ (format nil "~a ~a ~a" x y z))
        (terpri)
)

> (par-ex7 2 3)

> (par-ex7 3 4 5 6 7)

> (par-ex7 9 8 7)

> (defun par-ex8(&rest x)
      (princ x)
      (terpri)
)

> (par-ex8)

> (par-ex8 2 3 4)

> (par-ex8 8)

> (par-ex8 8 9)

> (par-ex8 '(1 2 3))

> (par-ex8 'a 'b 'c)

> (par-ex8 '(a b c))

Suppose the function **par-q3** is defined as follows.

(defun par-q3 (&rest x)
  (cond
    ((null x) "Nothing there")
    (t (cdr x))
)
)

What is returned by the following?

LESSON 9

(par-q3)

(par-q3 2)

(par-q3 2 3 4)

(par-q3 (+ 4 5))

(par-q3 3 4 5 6)

If no value is supplied for an **&rest** parameter, what value is used?

What is the type of an **&rest** parameter?

Write a function which has an arbitrary number of parameters and which returns a list of the numbers in the parameters. For example, if the function is named **list-nums**,

(list-nums 'a 3 4 'b 'c 9) => (3 4 9)

```
       Enter the following.
;; ** In the following function the tildes ( ~ ) at the
;; ** ends of the second and third lines are immediately
;; ** followed by <RET>.
>      (defun par-ex9 (a b &optional x y &rest r)
          (princ (format nil "Required   ~a ~a ~
                              ~%Optional  ~a ~a ~
                              ~%Rest      ~a"      a b x y r)
          )
          (terpri)
       )
```

> (par-ex9 1 2)

> (par-ex9 1 2 3)

> (par-ex9 1 2 3 4)

> (par-ex9 1 2 3 4 5)

> (par-ex9 1 2 3 4 5 6)

> (par-ex9 1 2 3 4 5 6 7 8)
;; ** In the next definition the tilde at the end of
;; ** the second line is followed immediately by <RET>.

> (defun par-ex10 (&optional (x 99) (y 999) &rest r)
          (princ (format nil "Optional ~a ~a ~
                       ~%Rest ~a" x y r)
)
          (terpri)
)

> (par-ex10)

> (par-ex10 8)

> (par-ex10 7 8)

> (par-ex10 1 2 3)

> (par-ex10 2 3 4 5 6)

> (par-ex10 'a 'b 'c)

> (par-ex10 '(a b c))

> (par-ex10 '(a b) '(c d))

> (par-ex10 nil nil '(a b c))

Suppose the function **par-q4** is defined as follows.

(defun par-q4 (&optional (listpart 'head) &rest r)
  (cond
    ((eq listpart 'head) (car r))
    ((eq listpart 'tail) (cdr r))
    (t r)
)
)

What is returned by the following uses of **par-q4**?

(par-q4)

(par-q4 'head)

(par-q4 'tail)

(par-q4 'whatever)

(par-q4 'head 1 2 3 4)

(par-q4 'tail 1 2 3 4)

(par-q4 'whatever 1 2 3 4)

(par-q4 'head 'head)

(par-q4 'head 'tail)

(par-q4 'tail 'tail)

(par-q4 'tail 'head)

(par-q4 'whatever 'whatever)

Describe the use of required, **&optional** and **&rest** parameters.

Why is the order for the types of parameters (first the required parameters, then the **&optional** parameters and then the **&rest** parameters) the logical one? That is, why wouldn't another ordering of parameters work?

Write a function which performs an arithmetic operation using two or more values. The first two parameters must always be present and evaluate to numbers. The third parameter, if present, must denote an arithmetic operation. Any additional parameters, if present, must evaluate to numbers. If just two values are supplied to the function, they must denote numbers to be added. After the two numbers an optional argument for the operation to be performed may be given. If the operation is not given, addition is to be used. If an operation is given it may be followed by additional numerical values whose sum added to the second argument supplied is to be used in doing the arithmetic operation. For example, if the function were named **f** then

(f 8 9) => 17   ; 17 = 8 + 9

(f 8 9 '*) => 72   ; 72 = 8 * 9

(f 8 5 '* 6) => 88   ; 88 = 8 * (5 + 6)

(f 10 9 '-) => 1   ; 1 = 10 - 9

(f 10 5 '- 3) => 2   ; 2 = 10 - (5 + 3)

(f 2.4 3.5) => 5.9   ; 5.9 = 2.4 + 3.5

(f 0.1 2 '/) => 0.05   ; 0.05 = 0.1 / 2

The symbols that may be used for the operation are + − * /. If the symbol for the operation to be performed is not one of these, the value **0** should be returned.

It may be helpful to write a function listsum which returns the sum of the numbers in a list.

Suppose Lisp only provided + for two numbers. For example, (+ 2 3) was legal but (+ 2 3 4) was not. Write a function which would add any number of numbers. (Of course, this function will need an **&rest** parameter.) It may be useful to use a local function.

SUMMARY

In the definition of functions, **&optional** provides a means of allowing some parameters to be left unspecified when the function is called.

Using **&rest** allows a programmer to have an arbitrary number of parameters to be passed to a function. These parameters are put in a list.

LESSON 10
Controlling Execution Flow (2)

Enter the following.

> (dolist (s '(a b c d e)) (princ s) (terpri))

> (dolist (s '(a b)) (princ s) (terpri))

> (dolist (s ()) (princ s) (terpri))

> (defun do-ex1 (L) (dolist (s L) (princ s)) (terpri)))

> (do-ex1 '(a b c d e))

> (do-ex1 ())

> (do-ex1 '((a b) (c d)))

> (do-ex1 (+ 1 2 3))

> (dolist (s '(a b c) 'done) (princ s) (terpri))

> (dolist (s '(hip hip) 'hooray) (princ s) (terpri))

> (defun do-ex2 (L)
    (dolist (s L (car L)) (princ s) (terpri))
)

LESSON 10

> (do-ex2 '(a b c))

> (do-ex2 '(go and))

> (do-ex2 '(run spot))

> (defun do-ex3 (L)
    (dolist (s L '!) (princ s) (princ " "))
)

> (do-ex3 '(run spot run))

> (defun do-ex4 (L)
    (let (r ())
      (dolist (s L r) (setf r (cons s r)))
)
)

> (do-ex4 '(a b c))

> (do-ex4   '(a b c d e f))

> (do-ex4 ())

> (do-ex4 '(a))

Suppose the function do-q1 is defined as follows.

(defun do-q1 (L)
  (let (c 0)
    (dolist (s L c) (setq c (+ c 1)))
)
)

What is returned by the following?

(do-q1 '(a b c))

(do-q1 '(a))

(do-q1 ())

What does the function **do-q1** do?

The function **do-ex1** was defined as follows.

(defun do-ex1 (L)
  (dolist (s L) (princ s)) (terpri))
)

Suppose it is changed by moving one parenthesis as follows.

(defun do-ex1 (L)
  (dolist (s L) (princ s) (terpri)))
)

What effect does this change have?

Suppose **whatever** is a function and **our-dolist** and **lisp-dolist** are functions defined as follows.

(defun our-dolist (L)
  (cond
    ((null L)) nil)
    (t (whatever (car L)) (our-dolist (cdr L)))
)
)

(defun lisp-dolist (L)
  (dolist (s L) (whatever s))
)

If **L** is a list, is there any difference between the effect of evaluating the following expressions?

(our-dolist L)

(lisp-dolist L)

Do they return the same value?

Use **dolist** to construct a function which takes one argument, a list, and returns a list consisting of the symbols in the list. For example,

(sym-list '(a b 1 2 (x y) c 3)) => **(A B C)**

The symbols in the list that is returned should be in the same order as they were in the original list. [Hint: **reverse** is useful.]

    Enter the following.

> (dotimes (i 10) (princ i) (terpri))

> (dotimes (i 10 'done) (princ i) (princ " "))

> (defun do-ex5 (n) (dotimes (i n) (princ i)))

> (do-ex5 5)

> (do-ex5 1)

> (do-ex5 0)

> (do-ex5 −1)

> (do-ex5 'a)

> (defun do-ex6 (n)
    (dotimes (i n 'done)
      (princ (format nil "~a   ~a~%" i (* i i)))
)
)

> (do-ex6 8)

> (do-ex6 12)

> (do-ex6 0)

> (do-ex6 −1)

> (do-ex6 'a)

```
> (dotimes (i 4)                                 ; This is a little perverse.
      (princ i)
      (terpri)
      (setf i (+ i 1))
      (princ i)
      (terpri)
  )

> (defun do-ex7 (n)
      (let ((L '()))
           (dotimes (i n L) (setq L (cons i L)))
      )
  )

> (do-ex7 5)

> (defun do-ex8 (n)
      (dolist (s (do-ex7 n)) (princ s) (terpri))
  )

> (do-ex8 5)

> (do-ex8 0)

> (defun do-ex9 (n)
      (dotimes (i n) (princ (- n (+ i 1))) (terpri))
  )

> (do-ex9 5)

> (do-ex9 0)

> (defun do-ex10 (m n)
      (dotimes (i m (terpri))
          (dotimes (j n (terpri))
              (princ (format nil "~a    ~a" i j))
          )
      )
  )

> (do-ex10 4 6)

> (do-ex10 6 4)

> (do-ex10 0 6)

> (do-ex10 5 0)
```

In **dotimes** what is the first value used in the loop?

In **dotimes** what is the last value used in the loop?

Suppose **do-q2** is defined as follows.

```
(defun do-q2 (n)
  (let ((s 0))
    (dotimes (i n s) (setq s (+ i s))
  )
)
```

What are the values of the following?

(do-q2 5)

(do-q2 1)

(do-q2 0)

Compare the functions **do-ex8** and **do-ex9**. Do they do the same thing? Which is easier to understand?

Use **dotimes** to write a function which returns a list of integers which starts at 1 and ends at the integer specified. For example, if the function is named **int-list**

(int-list 5) => (1 2 3 4 5)

Assuming **whatever** is a function which has an numeric argument, the expression

(dotimes (i n) (whatever i))

evaluates **(whatever i)** with an increasing sequence of values. Write an expression using **dotimes** which evaluates **(whatever i)** with the same values, but in decreasing order. [Hint: consider **do-ex9**.]

Enter the following.
The next function is defined as a matter of convenience. It might be worth saving.

```
>   (defun pr-sp (x)                          ; PRint with SPace
        (princ x) (princ " ")
    )

>   (do ((j 0 (+ j 1))) ((= j 10)) (pr-sp j))

>   (do ((j 0 (+ j 2))) ((= j 12)) (pr-sp j))

>   (defun do-ex11 (n)
        (do ((j 0 (+ j 1))) ((= j n))
            (princ j)
            (terpri)
        )
    )

>   (do-ex11 5)

>   (do-ex11 0)

>   (do ((j 0)) ((= j 10) 'done)
        (pr-sp j)
        (setf j (1+ j))
    )

>   (do ((j 0 (+ j 1))) ((= j 10) 'done) (pr-sp j))

>   (defun do-ex12 (n)
        (let ((s 0))
            (do ((j n (- j 1))) ((zerop j) s)
```

LESSON 10

```
                    (setq s (+ s j))
                )
           )
      )

> (do-ex12 9)

> (do-ex12 0)

> (defun do-ex13 (m)
      (do ((i 1 (* 2 i)) (j m (+ j 2))) ((> i j) 'done)
          (pr-sp i) (pr-sp j) (terpri)
      )
  )

> (do-ex13 4)

> (do-ex13 1000)

> (do-ex13 0)

> (defun do-ex14 (m)
      (do ((i 1 (* 2 i))
           (j m (+ j 2))
           (k 0 (+ k 10))
          )
          ((> i j) 'done)
          (pr-sp i) (pr-sp j) (pr-sp k) (terpri)
      )
  )

> (do-ex14 4)

> (do-ex14 1000)

> (do-ex14 0)

> (do ((x '(a b c))) ((null x))
      (pr-sp (car x))
      (setf x (cdr x))
  )

> (do ((x '(a b c) (cdr x))) ((null x))
      (pr-sp (car x))
  )

> (do ((x '(a b c) (cdr x))) ((null x) 'done)
      (pr-sp (car x))
  )
```

> (defun do-ex15 (L)
     (do ((x L (cdr x)) (y nil (cons (car x) y)))
         ((null x) 'done)
         (princ (format nil "~a   ~a~%" x y))
)
)

> (do-ex15 '(a b c))

> (do-ex15 '((a b) (c d)))

> (do-ex15 ())

> (defun do-ex16 (L)
     (do ((x L (cdr x)) (n 0 (+ n 1))) ((null x) n)))
)

What is the output produced by the following expression?

**(do ((j 5 (− j 1))) ((zerop j) 'done)
  (princ j) (terpri)
)**

Suppose **do-q3** is defined as follows.

**(defun do-q3 ()
  (do ((m 0 (1+ m)) (n 12 (1− n))) ((< n m))
    (princ (format nil "~a ~a~%" m n))
)
)**

What will **(do-q3)** print on the screen?

LESSON 10

Suppose **do-q4** is defined as follows.

```
(defun do-q4 (k)
  (do ((m 0 (+ m 1)) (n 1 (* 2 n))) ((= m k))
    (princ (format nil "~a ~a~%" m n))
  )
)
```

What will **(do-q4 3)** output to the screen?

Suppose **do-q5** is defined as follows.

```
(defun do-q5 (n)
  (do ((L nil (cons 'a L))
       (i n (- i 1))
      )
      ((zerop n) L))
)
```

What does **(do-q5 6)** return?

Suppose **L** is a list. Write an expression using **do** (and additional variables) which has the same effect as **(dolist (s L) (whatever s))**. Assume **whatever** is an appropriately defined function.

Suppose n is a positive number. Write an expression using **do** (and additional variables) which has the same effect as **(dotimes (i n) (whatever i))**. Assume whatever is an appropriately defined function.

Enter the following.
If the following function has been saved, just **load** it.

> (defun pr-sp (x) (princ x) (princ " "))   ; PRint with
                                                   ; SPace

> (setf n 6)

> (loop
      (pr-sp n)
      (setf n (− n 2))
      (if (zerop n) (return))
)

> (defun loop-ex1 (n)
      (loop
           (pr-sp n)
           (setf n (− n 1))
           (if (zerop n) (return))
)
)

> (loop-ex1 9)

> (loop-ex1 1)

> (defun loop-ex2 (L)
      (loop
           (pr-sp (car L))
           (setf L (cdr L))
           (if (null L) (return))
)
)

> (loop-ex2 '(a b c))

> (loop-ex2 '((a b) (c d)))

> (loop-ex2 nil)

> (defun loop-ex3 (L)
      (loop
           (pr-sp (car L))

LESSON 10

```
                    (setf L (cdr L))
                    (if (null L) (return 'empty))
              )
        )
```

> `(loop-ex3 '(a b c))`

> `(loop-ex3 '((a b) (c d)))`

> `(loop-ex3 '(a))`

> ```
  (defun loop-read-1 ()
       (loop
             (if (princ (read)) (terpri) (return))
)
)
  ```

> `(loop-read-1)`                           ; No value (or prompt) is returned
                                            ; immediately.   Enter the following
                                            ; expressions (one per line).

```
9
(a b c)
(+ 9 8)
(car '(a b c))
nil
```

              ;; ** The next line is entered as one.

> `(loop-read-1) 1 2 3 4 (a b c) nil`

> `(loop-read-1)`   ; No value (or prompt) is returned
                                            ; immediately.   Enter the following
                                            ; expressions here (one per line).

```
(setf x 10)
x
nil
```

> `(loop-read-1)`   ; No value (or prompt) is returned
                                            ; immediately.   Enter the following
                                            ; expressions here (one per line).

```
(defun square(x) (* x x))
(square 8)
nil
```

> `(loop-read-1)`   ; No value (or prompt) is returned
                                            ; immediately.   Enter the following
                                            ; expressions here (one per line).

```
(car '(a b c))
(cdr '(a))
```
```

nil

> (defun loop-read-2 ()
    (loop
        (if (princ (eval (read))) (terpri) (return))
)
)

> (loop-read-2)   ; No value (or prompt) is returned
                                         ; immediately.   Enter the following
                                         ; expressions here (one per line).
9
'(a b c)
(+ 9 8)
(car '(a b c))
nil
        ;; ** The next line is entered as one.

> (loop-read-2) 1 2 3 4 '(a b c)

> (loop-read-2)   ; No value (or prompt) is returned
                                         ; immediately.   Enter the following
                                         ; expressions here (one per line).
(setf x 10)
x
nil

> (loop-read-2)   ; No value (or prompt) is returned
                                         ; immediately.   Enter the following
                                         ; expressions here (one per line).
(defun square(x) (* x x))
(square 8)
nil

> (loop-read-2)   ; No value (or prompt) is returned
                                         ; immediately.   Enter the following
                                         ; expressions here (one per line).
(car '(a b c))
(cdr '(a))
nil

What does **loop** do?

What do you think would happen if the function **loop-ex1** (defined above) was invoked by **(loop-ex1 −1)**? Why? N.B. This may not be a good experiment to try.

What do you think would happen if **loop** was used without **return**? Why? N.B. This may not be a good experiment to try.

What is the difference between the functions **loop-read-1** and **loop-read-2** (defined above)?

The functions reader1 and reader2 (defined above) are written very tersely (on purpose). Do you think that this is a good idea? Did you find them hard to understand? Would you like them to have been written differently?

Enter the following.

```
>   (case 7
        ((1 2 3) 'in-first-three)
        ((4 6 8 10) 'small-even-number)
        ((3 5 7) 'small-odd-number)
    )
```

```
> (case 7
        (1    'first)
        (2    'second)
        (3    'third)
        ((4 5 6 7) 'also-ran)
  )

> (case 9
        (1    'first)
        (2    'second)
        (3    'third)
        ((4 5 6 7) 'also-ran)
  )

> (case 99
        (1 'first)
        (2 'second)
        (3 'third)
        ((4 5 6 7) 'also-ran)
        (otherwise 'did-not-finish)
  )

> (defun case-ex1 (n)
      (case n
          (1 'first)
          (2 'second)
          (3 'third)
          ((4 5 6 7) 'also-ran)
          (otherwise 'did-not-finish)
      )
  )

> (case-ex1 9)

> (case-ex1 1)

> (case-ex1 0)

> (case-ex1 'x)

> (defun case-ex2 (n)
     (case n
         (1 (princ "GREAT JOB") (terpri)
            (princ "SUPER!!") (terpri) 'first)
         (2 (princ "CONGRATULATIONS") (terpri) 'second)
         (3 (princ "NICE GOING") (terpri) 'third)
         ((4 5 6 7) (princ "NICE TRY") (terpri) 'also-ran)
         (otherwise)
     )
  )
```

LESSON 10   **121**

> (case-ex2 1)

> (case-ex2 2)

> (case-ex2 3)

> (case-ex2 4)

> (case-ex2 5)

> (case-ex2 100)

> (case-ex2 'x)

What are the values of the following expression?

```
(case 'e
  ((a e i o u) 'vowel)
  (y 'vowel-or-consonant)
  (otherwise 'consonant)
)

(case 'f
  ((a e i o u) 'vowel)
  (y 'vowel-or-consonant)
  (otherwise 'consonant)
)

(case 'y
  ((a e i o u) 'vowel)
  (y 'vowel-or-consonant)
  (otherwise 'consonant)
)

(case 'whats-this
  ((a e i o u) 'vowel)
  (y 'vowel-or-consonant)
  (otherwise 'consonant)
)
```

What value is returned by a **case** expression if none is is given for the value that follows **case**?

Write the following expression using **cond** instead of **case**.

```
(case x
  (1 'one)
  (2 'two)
  (3 'third)
  ((4 5 6) 'middle)
  (otherwise 'unknown)
)
```

SUMMARY

Lisp provides several looping constructs. **Dolist** iterates through the elements of a list. **Dotimes** sequences through numerical values. **Do** and the **loop return** combination are general loop constructs.

Case provides a multiway selection structure.

LESSON 11
Using Functions

Enter the following.

> ((lambda (x) (* 2 x)) 5)   ; The first part of this
                                   ; (all but the 5) is called
                                   ; a lambda-expression.

> (defun double (x) (* 2 x))

> (describe 'double)

> (double 5)

Compare the function definition of **double** with the lambda-expression that precedes it.

> (setq x 10)

> ((lambda (x) (* 2 x)) 4)

> x

123

> ((lambda (x) (* 2 x)) x)

> x

> ((lambda (x) (* 2 x)) (+ 3 x))

> x

> ((lambda (e L) (cons e L)) 'a '(x y z))

> ((lambda (e L) (cons e L)))

> ((lambda (e L) (cons e L)) 'a '(b c d) '(x y z))

> (setq L '(a b c d e))

> ((lambda (e L) (cons e L)) L L)

> (append ((lambda (e L) (cons e L)) L L) L)

> (function (lambda (x) (* 2 x)))

> #'(lambda (x) (* 2 x))

> (function double)

> #'double

> (equal (function double) #'double)

> (equal (function double)
        (function (lambda (x) (* 2 x)))
)

> (functionp #'double)

> (functionp #'triple)

> (functionp double)

> (setq double 2)

> (functionp double)

> (functionp (function double))

> (functionp #'double)

LESSON 11

> (defun 4thpower (x)
>   ((lambda (y) (* y y)) (* x x))
>)

> (4thpower 3)

> (4thpower 8)

> (4thpower (4thpower 2))

What are the values of the following expressions?

((lambda (x) (car (cdr x))) '(a b c d))   6

((lambda (x) (+ (car x) (cadr x))) '(1 2 3 4))   3

((lambda (x) (numberp (car x))) '(a b c d))   nil

((lambda (x) (listp x)) '(a b c d))   t

Explain how the function **4thpower** (defined above) works.

Are the variables that follow **lambda** in a lambda-expression local or global references?

What is the relation between **#'** and **function**?

Enter the following.

> (funcall car '(a b c))

> (funcall 'car '(a b c))

> (funcall #'car '(a b c))

> (setq L '(a b c d e))

> (funcall #'car L)

> (funcall #'cdr L)

> (funcall #'cons 'x '(a b c))

> (funcall #'list 'a 'b 'c 'd)

> (funcall #'append '(a) '(b) '(c))

> (funcall #'+ 2 3 4)

> (funcall #'- 4 3 2)

> (funcall #'(lambda (x) (* 2 x)) 4)

> (funcall #'(lambda (x) (* x x)) (+ 3 4 5 6))

> (funcall #'(lambda (&rest L) (car L)) 'a 'b 'c)

> (defun double (x) (* 2 x))

> (funcall #'double 3)

> (defun list-op(f L) (funcall f L))

> (list-op 'car '(a b c))

> (list-op #'car '(a b c))

> (list-op (function car) '(a b c))

> (list-op 'cdr '(a b c d))

> (list-op #'cdr '(a b c d))

> (list-op (function cdr) '(a b c d))

> (list-op #'car L)

> (list-op #'cdr L)

> (list-op #'(lambda (x) (cons (car x) x)) L)

LESSON 11

```
>   (defun snoc (L x)                       ; This will be handy.
        (append L (list x))
    )

>   (snoc '(a b c) 99)                      ; Check

>   (defun rotate (L)
        (snoc (cdr L) (car L))
    )

>   (rotate L)                              ; Check

>   (list-op #'rotate L)

>   (list-op #'rotate (list-op #'rotate L))

>   (defun put-first (test L)
        (cond
            ((null L) ())
            ((funcall test (car L))
                (cons (car L) (put-first test (cdr L)))
            )
            (t   (snoc (put-first test (cdr L)) (car L)))
        )
    )

>   (put-first #'symbolp '(a 1 b 2))

>   (put-first #'numberp '(a 1 b 2))

>   (setq L '(a b c 1 2 3 (x y) (r s)))

>   (put-first #'symbolp L)

>   (put-first #'atom L)

>   (put-first #'listp L)

>   (put-first #'numberp L)

>   (put-first #'stringp L)

>   (defun put-numbers-first (L)
        (put-first #'numberp L)
    )

>   (put-numbers-first '(1 a 2 b))

>   (put-numbers-first L)
```

{ rotate ??

> (defun put-atoms-first (L)
>   (put-first #'atom L)
>   )

> (put-atoms-first '(a (x y) b "HELLO" c))

> (put-atoms-first L)

Give the values of the following expressions.

(funcall #'cons 'x '(a b c))

(funcall #'list 'a 'b 'c 'd)

(funcall #'append '(a) '(b) '(c))

(funcall #'− 4 3 2)

(funcall #'(lambda (x y) (* x x y)) (+ 2 3) 4)

There are places where either **'some-function, #'some-function** or **(function some-function)** may be used. Which do you think is preferable (and why)?

Use **put-first** (as defined above) to define a function **put-lists-first** which has one argument, a list, and which returns a list consisting of the same objects as the orginal list, but with the lists of the list given first.

Define a function called **filter** which has two arguments. The first argument is a predicate and the second is a list. **Filter** returns the list of elements of the list which satisfy the predicate. For example,

(filter #'numberp '(a 1 b 2 3) => (1 2 3)

(filter #'symbolp '((x y) a b c (f g))) => (A B C)

LESSON 11

Enter the following.

```
>   (apply #'+ '(2 3 4))
>   (apply #'list '(a b c d))
>   (apply #'- '(3 4 5))
>   (apply #'cons '(a (x y z)))
>   (apply #'append '((a b) (x y)))
>   (apply #'+ (list 1 2 3 4 5))
>   (defun arith-op (op &rest L)
        (apply op L)
    )
>   (arith-op #'+ 1 2 3 4)
>   (arith-op #'* 2 3 4 5)
>   (arith-op #'list 'a 'b 'c)
>   (defun snoc (L x)
        (append L (list x))
    )
>   (snoc '(a b c) 3)                    ; Check
>   (defun put-first (test L)
        (cond
            ((null L) ())
            ((apply test (list (car L)))
                (cons (car L) (put-first test (cdr L)))
            )
            (t    (snoc (put-first test (cdr L)) (car L)))
        )
    )
```

> (put-first #'numberp '(a b 1 2 c 4))

> (put-first #'symbolp '(a b 1 2 c 4))

What are the values of the following expresssions?

(apply #'+ '(8 2 1))

(apply #'list '(a b c d))

(apply #'cons '(a (x y z)))

(apply #'car '((a b c)))

Contrast **apply** and **funcall**.

Enter the following.

> (mapcar 'zerop '(1 0 2 0 0 3))

> (mapcar #'zerop '(1 0 2 0 0 3))

> (defun triple(x) (* 3 x))

> (mapcar #'triple '(0 2 4 6 8))

> (mapcar #'(lambda(x) (* 2 x)) '(1 3 5 7))

> (mapcar #'+ '(1 2 3 4) '(10 20 30))

> (mapcar #'+ '(1 2 3) '(10 20 30 40 50))

> (setq L '(1 2 3 4 5))

> (mapcar #'+ L L '(10 20 30 40))

> (mapcar #'+ '(100) L)

> (mapcar #'* L L L L)

LESSON 11

> (mapcar #'list '(a b c d e) '(1 2 3) '(p q r s t u))

> (mapcar #'cons '(a b c d e f)
       '((1 2 3) (4 5 6 7) (8 9 10))
)

> (mapcar #'cons L (list L L L L L L L))

> (mapcar #'list L L L)

> (mapcar #'list L (cdr L) (cddr L))

What are the values of the following expressions?

(mapcar #'+ '(1 2 3) '(10 20))

(mapcar #'+ '(1 2 3) '(10 20 30 40))

(mapcar #'+ '(1 2 3 4) '(10 20 30)
    '(100 200 300 400)
)

(mapcar #'car '((a b) (c d e) (f) (g h i)))

(mapcar #'list '(a b c) '(1 2 3 4) '(x y z))

(mapcar #'numberp '(1 a 2 w 3 (x y z) 4))

Enter the following.

> (maplist #'cdr '(a b c d e))

> (maplist #'car '(a b c d))

> (maplist #'caar '((a b) (c d e) (x y z)))

> (maplist #'(lambda (L) (cons 'aa L)) '(a b c d))

> (maplist #'atom '(a b (c d) 1 2 (x y)))

> (maplist #'listp '(a b c 1 2 3))

> (defun 2car(L)
      (cond
         ((numberp (car L)) (* 2 (car L)))

```
        (t 0)
    )
)
```
> (maplist #'2car '(1 a v 3 y))

What are the values of the following expressions?

(maplist #'cddr '(a b c d))

(maplist #'cadr '(a b c d))

(maplist #'(lambda (L) (cons (car L) (cddr L)))
   '(a b c d)
)

(maplist #'length '(a b c d))

SUMMARY

Lambda provides a means of defining a function without a name.

Function and **#'** are used to access function definitions.

Functionp is a predicate for testing whether an expression is a function.

Funcall and **apply** cause a function to be used with arguments.

Mapcar and **maplist** cause a function to be used with lists.

LESSON 12
List Manipulation (3)

Enter the following.

> (last '(1 2 3 4))

> (butlast '(1 2 3 4))

> (setq L '(a b c d e f g h i j k l m n o p))

> (last L)

> (butlast L)

> (butlast L 1)

> (butlast L 2)

> (butlast L 13)

> (butlast L 20)

> (subseq L 3)

> (subseq L 0)

> (subseq L 9)

> (subseq L 20)

> (subseq L 2 4)

> (subseq L 5 10)

> (subseq L 3 3)

> (subseq L 10 20)

> (elt L 2)

> (elt L 5)

> (elt L 0)

> (elt L 20)

> (elt (subseq L 3) 2)

> (nth 2 L)

> (nth 5 L)

> (nth 0 L)

> (nth 20 L)

> (setf (elt L 2) 20)

> L

> (setf (elt L 4) 40)

> L

> (setf (subseq L 7 9) '(70 80 90))

> L

Suppose the value of **L** is **'(10 20 30 40 50 60 70 80 90)** . What are the values of the following?

(last L)

(butlast L 3)

(butlast (butlast L 2) 3)

(subseq L 3)

(subseq L 7)

(subseq L 2 4)

(subseq (butlast L 2) 3 5)

(elt L 4)

(nth 2 L)

(elt (subseq L 3 5) 2)

If **L** is a list, what is an expression using **subseq** which returns the same value as **(cdr L)**?

If **L** is a list, what is an expression using **elt** which returns the same value as **(car L)**?

If **L** is a list, what is an expression using **elt** and **setf** which has the same effect as **(rplaca L x)**?

Enter the following.

> (setq L '(a b c d e f g h i j k l a b a b))
> (remove 'a L)
> L
> (remove 'f L)

> L

> (remove 'z L)

> L

> (remove 'a L :start 3)

> (remove 'a L :start 5 :end 7)

> (remove 'a L :count 1)

> (remove 'a L :count 2)

> (remove 'a L :start 3 :count 2)

> (delete 'p L)

> L

> (delete 'b L)

> L

> (delete 'z L)

> L

> (substitute 'z 'a L)

> L

> (substitute 'x 'b L)

> L

> (substitute 'v 'w L)

> L

> (setq L '(a b a b a b c d a b c d))

> (substitute 'z 'a L)

> L

> (substitute 'z 'a L :start 1)

> (substitute 'z 'a L :start 3)

LESSON 12

> (substitute 'z 'a L :start 1 :end 5)
> (substitute 'x 'c L :start 2 :end 6)
> (substitute 'z 'a L :count 1)
> (substitute 'z 'a L :count 2)
> (substitute 'z 'a L :start 3 :count 2)
> (substitute 'z 'a L :start 3 :end 5 :count 4)
> (substitute 'z 'a L :start 2 :end 9 :count 2)
> (setq L '(a 1 a 2 a 3 a 4 b 5 b 6 b 7 c 8 d 9))
> (position 'a L)
> (position 'b L)
> (position 'c L)
> (position 'z L)
> (position 'a L :from-end t)
> (position 'b L :from-end t)
> (position 'c L :from-end t)
> (position 'a L :start 10)
> (position 'a L :start 3)
> (position 'b L :start 4)
> (position 'b L :start 2 :end 6)
> (count 'a L)
> (count 'b L)
> (count 'c L)
> (count 'z L)
> (count 'a L :start 2)
> (count 'a L :start 7)

> (count 'a L :start 2 :end 5)

> (count 'a L :start 5 :end 12)

> (find 'a L)

> (find 'b L)

> (find 'z L)

> (find 'a L :start 4)

> (find 'a L :start 10)

> (find 'b L :start 4 :end 14)

> (find 'b L :start 2 :end 5)

Suppose L is the list '(1 2 3 4 5 1 2 3 4 5 6 7 8 9 1 2 3). What are the values of the following?

(remove 2 L)

(remove 2 L :count 2)

(remove 2 L :start 4)

(remove 2 L :start 4 :end 8)

(substitute 20 2 L)

(position 3 L)

(position 3 L :start 5)

(position 5 L :from-end t)

(count 4 L)

(count 4 L :start 7)

The function **remove** is called nondestructive, while the function **delete** is called destructive. Why?

LESSON 12

Enter the following.

> (defun car=a(x) (equal (car x) 'a))   ; For use in what
                                              ; follows.

> (car=a '(a b))   ; Check

> (car=a '(b a))   ; Another check

> (setq LL
        '((a b) (a c) (b c) (b d) (b e) (a b c) (c b)
          (x y z) 1 2)
)

> (find-if #'car=a LL)

> (find-if #'car=a LL :start 1)

> (find-if #'car=a LL :start 2)

> (find-if #'car=a LL :start 6)

> (find-if #'car=a LL :start 3 :end 5)

> (find-if #'listp LL)

> (find-if #'numberp LL)

> (find-if #'symbolp LL)

> (position-if #'car=a LL)

> (position-if #'car=a LL :start 1)

> (position-if #'car=a LL :start 2)

> (position-if #'car=a LL :start 3 :end 5)

> (position-if #'car=a LL :from-end t)

> (position-if #'listp LL)

> (position-if #'numberp LL)

> (count-if #'car=a LL)

> (count-if #'car=a LL :start 1)

> (count-if #'car=a LL :start 2)

> (count-if #'listp LL)

> (count-if #'numberp LL)

> (count-if #'symbolp '(a b c (x y z) 1 2 3 d e))

Suppose **L** has the value '(1 3 5 4 6 7 9 8 2). What are the values of the following? (**Evenp** is a Lisp predicate which is **t** when its argument is an even number.)

(find-if #'evenp L)

(find-if #'evenp L :start 2)

(find-if #'evenp L :start 0 :end 2)

(position-if #'evenp L)

(position-if #'evenp L :start 6)

(position-if #'evenp L :from-end t)

(count-if #'evenp L)

(count-if #'evenp L :start 7)

Suppose **L** is a list and **testp** is a predicate. If the value of (**count-if #'testp L**) is **0**, what is the value of (**position-if #'testp L**)?

Enter the following.

> (sort '(2 5 3 6 1 7) #'<)

> (sort '() #'<)

LESSON 12

> (defun car< (L1 L2) (< (car L1) (car L2)))   ; Used
                                                ; below

> (car< '(1 2 3) '(9 8 7))   ; Check

> (car< '(9 8 7) '(1 2 3))   ; Another check

> (sort '((2 7 z) (3 5 y) (1 2 x) (5 4) (9 3 a)) #'car<)

> (sort '((2 4 6 8) (1 3 5 7) (10 20 30 40 50)) #'car<)

> (setq L '(9 3 5 4 6 2))

> (sort L #'<)

> L

> (setq LL '((2 b) (5 e) (3 c) (9 i) (4 d) (1 a)))

> (sort LL 'car<)

> LL

> (sort '((3 c e) (1 a c) (2 b) (4 d f)) #'< :key 'car)

> (sort '((e 5) (b 2) (c 3) (a 1)) #'< :key #'cadr)

> (sort '(((5 e)) ((2 b)) ((3 c))) #'< :key #'caar)

> (sort '((3 c 4) (1 a 2) (2 b 7)) #'< :key #'third)

What are the values of the following expressions?

(sort '(2 3 4 1 5) #'<)

(sort '((2 4) (5 1) (3 6) (1 3)) #'< :key #'first)

(sort '((2 4) (5 1) (3 6) (1 3)) #'< :key #'cadr)

Does **sort** seem to be a destructive function?

Enter the following.

> (member 5 '(1 3 5 7 9))

> (setq s '(a b c d e f g h i j k l m n o p))

> (member 'a s)

> (member 'g s)

> (member 'z s)

> (union '(a b c d) s)

> (union '(a e i o u) s)

> (union s '(x y z))

> (union s s)

> (union s ())

> (intersection '(a b c) s)

> (intersection '(a e i o u) s)

> (intersection s '(x y z))

> (intersection s s)

> (intersection s ())

> (adjoin 'a s)

> s

> (adjoin 'x s)

> s

> (adjoin 'a nil)

> (subsetp '(a b c) s)

> (subsetp '(c b a) s)

> (subsetp '(a e i o u) s)

> (subsetp s ())

> (subsetp () s)

LESSON 12

> (remove-duplicates '(a a b c b))

> (setq s '(a a b c b))

> (remove-duplicates s)

> s

> (delete-duplicates '(a a b c b))

> (setq s '(a a b c b))

> (delete-duplicates s)

> s

What are the values of the following expressions?

(member 1 '(1 3 5))

(member 2 '(1 3 5))

(union '(1 3 5 7) '(2 3 4))

(union '(1 2) '(3 4 5))

(intersection '(1 3 5 7) '(2 3 4))

(intersection '(1 2) '(3 4 5))

(adjoin 1 '(1 3 5))

(adjoin 2 '(1 3 5))

(subsetp '(2 4) '(2 4 6 8))

(subsetp '(2 3 4) '(2 4 6 8))

(remove-duplicates '(1 1 3 4 3))

(delete-duplicates '(1 1 3 4 3))

Using **cond**, **car**, **cdr**, **eql**, **t**, **nil** and **null** only, define a function which has two parameters, an object and a list, that returns the same value as **member**.

What is the difference between the functions **adjoin** and **cons**?

SUMMARY

Lisp provides a variety of list manipulating functions. Some (**last, butlast, subseq, elt, nth**) return part of a list. Others modify the list (**remove, delete, substitute, sort**).

There are inquiry functions for lists (**position, count, find,** and so on) which determine the presence (or number of) certain values.

The behavior of these functions can be modified by using keyword parameters (**:start:, :end, :count, :key, :from-end**). Lisp can manipulate lists as sets with certain functions (**member, union, intersection, adjoin, subsetp**).

LESSON 13
Program Constructs

Enter the following.

```
>   (defun simpl-print (x)                  ; For later use.
        (princ (format nil "~%~a~%" x))     ; x will be on a
    )                                       ; line by itself.

>   (block b1
        (simpl-print "Start")
        (simpl-print "End")
    )

>   (block b2
        (simpl-print "Start")
        (return-from b2)
        (simpl-print "End")
    )

>   (block b3
        (simpl-print "Start")
        (return-from b3 'returning)
        (simpl-print "End")
    )

>   (setq x 10)
```

```
> (block b4
      (simpl-print "Start")
      (if (numberp x) (return-from b4 (* 2 x)))
      (simpl-print "End")
  )

> (block b5
      (simpl-print "Start")
      (if (listp x) (return-from b5 (* 2 x)))
      (simpl-print "End")
  )

> (defun blk-ex1 (x)
      (block b-1
          (cond
              ((null x) (return-from b-1 "Nothing here"))
              ((numberp x) (simpl-print "Number found"))
              (t (return-from b-1))
          )
      )
  )

> (blk-ex1 9)

> (blk-ex1 nil)

> (blk-ex1 'a)

> (defun blk-ex2 (x)
      (block b-2
          (simpl-print "At begin of block")
          (cond
              ((null x) (return-from b-2))
              ((numberp x) (if (zerop x)
                              (return-from b-2 0)
                              (simpl-print "Number found"))
              )
              ((listp x) (return-from b-2 (car x)))
              (t (simpl-print "At end of cond"))
          )
          (simpl-print "At end of block")
      )
      (simpl-print x)
  )

> (blk-ex2 nil)

> (blk-ex2 0)
```

LESSON 13

```
> (blk-ex2 9)

> (blk-ex2 '(a b c))

> (blk-ex2 "Hello")

> (blk-ex2 'a)

> (block b
      (dolist (x '(a b c z d e f z))
          (if (eql x 'z) (return-from b))
          (simpl-print x)
      )
  )

> (block b
      (loop
          (return-from b)
      )
  )

> (block b
      (let (x (L '(a b c z d e f z)))
          (loop
              (setq x (car L))
              (if (eql x 'z) (return-from b))
              (simpl-print x)
              (setq L (cdr L))
          )
      )
  )
```

What is printed (not returned) by the following expressions?

```
(block q1
   (princ "Hello") (terpri)
   (princ "Goodbye") (terpri)
)

(block q2
   (princ "Hello") (terpri)
   (return-from q2)
   (princ "Goodbye") (terpri)
)
```

What are the values returned by the following expressions?

```
(block q3
  (setq x 10)
  (if (numberp x) (return-from q3 (* 2 x)))
  (setq x 30)
)

(block q4
  (setq x 10)
  (if (numberp x) (return-from q4 (* 2 x))
                  (return-from q4 (* 7 x)))
  (setq x 30)
)

(block q5
  (setq x 'ten)
  (if (numberp x) (return-from q5 (* 2 x))
                  (return-from q5 0))
  (setq x 30)
)
```

What is the purpose of **block**?

Should the expression **(return-from bb)** occur outside of a block named **bb**?

Enter the following.

```
> (tagbody
    (setq L '(a b c d e f))
  again
    (if (eql (car L) 'd) (go out))
    (print (car L))
    (setq L (cdr L))
    (go again)
```

```
         out
              (print L)
         )
>  (let ((L '(a b c z d e f z)))
        (tagbody
            again
                 (if (eql (car L) 'z) (go out))
                 (print (car L))
                 (setq L (cdr L))
                 (go again)
            out
                 (print L)
        )
   )

>  (defun tag-ex (x)
        (tagbody
            again
                 (when (null x) (print 'done) (go out))
                 (when (listp x) (go list-tag))
                 (when (numberp x)
                     (print x)
                     (setq x (* x x))
                     (go num-tag)
                 )
                 (print x)
            num-tag
                 (setq x (list x))
                 (go again)
            list-tag
                 (print x)
                 (setq x (cdr x))
                 (go again)
            out
        )
   )

>  (tag-ex nil)

>  (tag-ex '(a b c))

>  (tag-ex 'a)

>  (tag-ex 4)

>  (tag-ex "HELLO")
```

What is printed (not returned) by the following expressions?

```
(tagbody
  (setq L '(1 2 3))
 again
    (if (eql (car L) 2) (go out))
    (princ (car L))
    (setq L (cdr L))
    (go again)
 out
    (princ L)
)

(let ((sum 0) (L '(1 2 3 4 5 6)))
  (tagbody
   again
     (if (eql sum 10) (go out))
     (setq sum (+ sum (car L)))
     (setq L (cdr L))
     (go again)
   out
     (princ sum)
  )
)
```

The function **tag-ex** given above is only for illustrating what **tagbody** permits and is a very poor example of programming style. Rewrite **tag-ex** so no **tagbody** or **go** is used. Use auxiliary functions if necessary.

Enter the following.

```
> (catch 'c1
    (if (numberp 3) (throw 'c1 7))
```

LESSON 13

```
          (throw 'c1 9)
      )

>   (catch 'c2
          (if (listp 3) (throw 'c2 7))
          (throw 'c2 9)
      )

>   (catch 'c3
          (if (numberp 3) (throw 'c3))
          (throw 'c3)
      )

>   (catch 'c4
          (if (listp 3) (throw 'c4))
          (throw 'c4)
      )

>   (setq x 99)

>   (catch 'c5
          (if (numberp 3) (throw 'c5 7))
          (setq x (* 2 4))
        )

>   x

>   (catch 'c6
          (if (listp 3) (throw 'c6 7))
          (setq x (* 3 11))
        )

>   x

>   (catch 'c7
          (if (listp 3) (throw 'c7 7))
          (throw 'c7 9)
          (setq x (* 3 5))
        )

>   x

>   (catch 'c8
          (if (listp 3) (throw 'c8))
          (throw 'c8)
          (setq x (* 2 9))
        )
      )
```

> x

> (defun simpl-print (x)   ; As earlier. If
      (princ (format nil "~%~a~%" x))   ; you haven't quit
)   ; since starting
                                            ; this lesson, this
                                            ; will still exist.

> (defun c-t-ex1 (x)
     (catch 'escape
        (if (not (null x)) (simpl-print "OK so far"))
        (if (numberp x) (throw 'escape (* 2 x)))
        (simpl-print "Number not found")
        (if (listp x) (throw 'escape (car x)))
        (simpl-print "Not a list")
        'exit-value
)
)

> (c-t-ex1 9)

> (c-t-ex1 nil)

> (c-t-ex1 'a)

> (defun c-t-ex2 (x)   ; Throws from all over
     (catch 'escape   ; (wild throws)
        (let ((L '(a b c)))
           (cond
              ((null x) (throw 'escape 'nothing-here))
              ((numberp x)
                 (if (zerop x) (throw 'escape 0)
                    (simpl-print x)
)
)
              ((listp x)
                 (if (eql (car x) (car L)) (throw 'escape (car x))
                    (simpl-print x)
)
)
              (t (simpl-print "end of cond"))
)
)
)
)

> (c-t-ex2 nil)

> (c-t-ex2 0)

LESSON 13

> (c-t-ex2 'a)

> (c-t-ex2 '(a b c))

> (c-t-ex2 9)

> (c-t-ex2 "Hello")

What are the values of the following expressions?

```
(catch 'q1
  (let ((L '(a b c)))
    (if (listp L) (throw 'q1 (car L)))
    (throw 'q1 (cdr L))
  )
)

(catch 'q2
  (let ((L '(a b c)))
    (if (symbolp L) (throw 'q2 L)))
    (throw 'q2 'not-a-symbol))
  )
)

(catch 'q3
  (let ((L '(a b c)))
    (if (listp L) (throw 'q3)))
    (throw 'q3 'not-a-symbol))
  )
)
```

What value is returned from a **throw** is none is supplied?

Enter the following.

> (defun simpl-print (x)   ; As before.
    (princ (format nil "~%~a~%" x))
)

> (prog ()
    (simpl-print "Hello")

```
        (simpl-print "Goodbye")
   )

>  (prog (x)
        (simpl-print x)
   )

>  (prog ((x 10))
        (simpl-print x)
   )

>  x

>  (prog ((x 10) v)
        (simpl-print x)
        (simpl-print v)
   )

>  (prog ((x 10) (v 5))
        (simpl-print x)
        (simpl-print v)
   )

>  (prog ((x 10) (v 5))
        (setq x (* x v))
        (simpl-print x)
     )

>  x

>  (setq c 100)

>  (prog (c)
        (simpl-print c)
   )

>  c

>  (prog (y)
        (simpl-print (boundp y))
   )

>  (prog ()
        (simpl-print "Before return. ")
        (return 123)
        (simpl-print "After return")
   )
```

LESSON 13

> (prog ((x 10))
    (simpl-print "Started")
    (if (numberp x) (return))
    (simpl-print "Ending")
)

> (prog ((x 10))
    (simpl-print "Started")
    (if (numberp x) (return x))
    (simpl-print "Ending")
    (return 123)
)

> (prog ((x 'ten))
    (simpl-print "Started")
    (if (numberp x) (return x))
    (simpl-print "Ending")
    (return 123)
)

> (setf m 'million)

> m

> (prog((x 10) (v 5))
    (return (+ x v))
    (setf m 1000)
)

> m

> (prog((x 10) (v 5))
    (setf m 1000)
    (return (+ x v))
)

> m

What is printed (not returned) by the following expressions?

(prog ((L '(a b c))
  (princ (car L)) (terpri)
  (if (null L) return)
  (princ "Here we are.") (terpri)
)

(prog (L)
  (princ (cons 'a L)) (terpri

```
            (if (null L) return)
            (princ "Here we are.") (terpri)
        )
```

If there is no **return** within a **prog** what value is returned by the **prog**?

When **return** is used within a **prog**, what value is returned by the **prog**?

What happens after the **return** within a **prog** is evaluated?

Enter the following.

```
> (defun go-ex(n)
      (prog()
          again
              (if (zerop n) (return (format nil "DONE ~%")))
              (princ n)
              (terpri)
              (setf n (1− n))
              (go again)
          (princ "AFTER GO")
          (terpri)
          (princ "ENDING")
      )
  )

> (go-ex 9)

> (go-ex (+ 3 4))

> (defun go-ex2(n)
      (prog()
          again
              (princ (format nil "~a before return~%" n))
```

LESSON 13

```
                (if (zerop n) (return (format nil "DONE")))
                (setf n (1− n))
                (princ (format nil "~a before go~%" n))
                (go again)
          )
    )
> (go-ex2 4)

> (defun go-ex3(alist)
       (prog()
           again
               (if (null alist) (return "DONE"))
               (princ (format nil "~a~%" (car alist)))
               (setf alist (cdr alist))
               (go again)
          )
    )
> (go-ex3 '(a b c))

> (go-ex3 '((a b) (c d)))

> (setf abclist '(a b c))

> (go-ex3 abclist)

> abclist
```

What does the function **go-ex3** when its argument is a list?

What does the following function do when its argument is a list?

```
(defun go-question (L)
   (prog()
     again
       (cond
         ((null L) (return))
         ((listp (car L))
            (princ (format nil "~%~a~%" (car L)))
         )
         (t (princ (format nil "~a " (car L))))
       )
```

```
        (setf L (cdr L))
        (go again)
   )
)
```

Compare **prog** with **let**, **block**, and **tagbody**. In particular, if **let**, **block** and **tagbody** are available is **prog** needed?

SUMMARY

Several Lisp constructs group Lisp statements together and have means of exiting: **block** with **return-from**, **tagbody** with **go**, **catch** with **throw** and **prog** with **return**, and **go**.

LESSON 14
Streams

```
;; ** This lesson is somewhat implementation dependent.
;; ** The comment "Enter ... " means no prompt will
;; ** appear but an input is needed. Enter an object
;; ** as indicated. Follow entries with <RET>.
```

Enter the following.

```
> (describe *standard-input*)

> (streamp *standard-input*)

> (input-stream-p *standard-input*)

> (output-stream-p *standard-input*)

> (stream-element-type *standard-input*)

> (type-of *standard-input*)

> (read *standard-input*)              ; Enter something.

> (symbolp (read *standard-input*))    ; Enter X.

> (listp (read *standard-input*))      ; Enter (A B C).

> (car (read *standard-input*))        ; Enter (A B C).
```

> (read *standard-input*)   ; Enter (+ 2 4).

> (numberp (read *standard-input*))   ; Enter (+ 2 4).

> (dotimes(i 5)
      (setq x (read *standard-input*))
      (princ x)
      (terpri)
)
                                              ; Enter 5 items here, one per line.

Does **(read *standard-input*)** cause the evaluation of the object that is input?

To what input device does ***standard-input*** refer?

Compare **(read)** and **(read *standard-input*)**.

Enter the following.

> (describe *standard-output*)

> (streamp *standard-output*)

> (input-stream-p *standard-output*)

> (output-stream-p *standard-output*)

> (stream-element-type *standard-output*)

> (type-of *standard-output*)

> (dolist (x '(a b c d e)) (princ x *standard-output*))

> (dotimes(i 10) (princ i *standard-output*))

> (dolist (x '(a bb ccc dddd))

LESSON 14

```
            (princ x *standard-output*)
            (terpri *standard-output*)
    )
>   (format *standard-output* "Hello")

>   (format *standard-output* "~a~%" "Goodbye")

>   (null
        (format *standard-output* "Hi ~%~%~%~% Bye~%")
    )

>   (dolist (x '(a b c d e))
        (format *standard-output* "~a~%" x)
    )

>   (defun a-format-ex (&rest L)
        (dolist (s L)
            (format *standard-output* "~6a ~10a ~6@a ~10@a ~%"
              s s s s)
        )
    )

>   (a-format-ex 'a 'bb 'ccc 'dddd 'eeee)

>   (a-format-ex nil '(a) '(a b) '(a b c))

>   (a-format-ex "A" "BE" "CAT" "DOOR" "FLARE")

>   (a-format-ex 1 21 321 4321 1.2 1.23 12.34 −1 −12)

>   (dolist (s '("A" "BE" "CAT" "DOOR" "FLARE"))
        (format *standard-output* "~6a ~10a ~6@a ~10@a ~%"
          s s s s)
    )

>   (dolist (i '(1 12 123 1234 −1 −12 −123 −1234))
        (format *standard-output*
              "~6d ~8d ~8,'0d ~6@d ~8@d ~8,'0@d ~d ~%"
              i i i i i i i)
        )
    )

>   (dolist (x '(0.001 0.01 0.012 0.1 0.12 1 1.2 1.23
                1.234 12 12.3 12.34 12.345 123 123.4
                123.45 123.456 −0.001 −0.01 −0.012 −0.1
                −0.12 −1 −1.2 −1.23 −1.234 −12 −12.3
                −12.34 −12.345 −123 −123.4 −123.45
                −123.456)
```

)
(format *standard-output*
   "~8f ~12f ~8,2f ~12,2f ~12,4f ~,2f ~,4f ~%"
   x x x x x x x x)
)

To what output device does ***standard-output*** refer?

What is the value of **(format *standard-output* ...)**?

What is printed by the following expressions?

(format *standard-output* "~a ~5a ~%" 'q 'q)

(format *standard-output* "~a ~5a ~%" 'abc 'abc)

(format *standard-output* "~4d ~8d ~%" 123 123)

(format *standard-output* "6,2f ~8,4f ~%"
   12.346 12.346)

Using the examples preceding these exercises, describe the format directives ~**a**, ~**d**, and ~**f**. (Hint: a stands for ASCII, d for Decimal and f for float.)

Enter the following.

> (setf in-strm (make-synonym-stream '*standard-input*))

> (describe in-strm)

> (streamp in-strm)

> (dotimes(i 5) (princ (* 2 (read in-strm))) (terpri))

LESSON 14

```
                                        ; Enter five numbers here,
                                        ; one per line.
> (setq x (read in-strm))               ; Enter an item, followed
                                        ; by <RET>.

> x

> (numberp (read in-strm))              ; Enter an item, followed
                                        ; by <RET>.

> (numberp (read in-strm))              ; Enter an item, followed
                                        ; by <RET>.

> (listp (read in-strm))                ; Ditto

> (close in-strm)

> (read in-strm)                        ; Ditto

> (read)                                ; Ditto

> (read *standard-input*)               ; Ditto

> (setf out-strm
        (make-synonym-stream '*standard-output*)
  )

> (describe out-strm)

> (format out-strm "Hello there!~%~%")

> (format out-strm "~a~%" '(a b c d))

> (dotimes(i 5) (princ i out-strm) (terpri out-strm))

> (dotimes(i 5) (format out-strm "~a     ~a~%" i (* 2 i)))

> (close out-strm)

> (format out-strm "Hello there")

> (setf s-in
        (make-string-input-stream
            "ABCEFGHIJKLMNOPQRSTUVWXYZ")
  )

> (read s-in)
```

> (read s-in)

> (streamp s-in)
;; ** Enter the next lines as written.

> (setf s-in (make-string-input-stream "A
B
C
D
E"))

> (read s-in)

> (read s-in)

> (let (c)
      (loop
          (if (null (setq c (read s-in))) (return))
          (princ c)
          (terpri)
)
)

> (read s-in)

> (close s-in)

> (read s-in)

> (setf s-out (make-string-output-stream))

> (get-output-stream-string s-out)

> (format s-out "Here it is.")

> (get-output-stream-string s-out)

> (get-output-stream-string s-out)

> (format s-out "Here it is again.~%")

> (format s-out "Here it is yet another time.~%")

> (get-output-stream-string s-out)

> (princ "Hello" s-out)

> (get-output-stream-string s-out)

LESSON 14

> `(stringp (princ "Hello again" s-out))`

> `(get-output-stream-string s-out)`

> `(defun build ()`
        `(princ "Enter five items, one per line")`
        `(terpri)`
        `(dotimes (i 5)`
              `(princ (read) s-out)`
        `)`
        `(terpri)`
        `(princ (get-output-stream-string s-out))`
  `)`

> `(build)`   ; Enter five items, one per line.

> `(build)`   ; Ditto

> `(defun build2 ()`
        `(princ "—>")`
        `(cond`
              `((princ (read) s-out) (build2))`
              `(t 'done)`
        `)`
  `)`

> `(build2)`   ; Enter items, quit by entering NIL

> `(get-output-stream-string s-out)`

> `(build2)`   ; Enter items, quit by entering NIL.

> `(get-output-stream-string s-out)`

> `(close s-out)`

> `(get-output-stream-string s-out)`

What are the values of **s1** and **s2** after the following sequence of expressions is evaluated?

(setf strm-in (make-string-input-stream "abc
def
ghi
jkl"))

(setf s1 (read strm-in))

(setf s2 (read strm-in))

The first parameter to **read**, if present, must be an input stream. What is the default input stream (i.e. the input stream used when none is specified)? What does it mean to describe an input stream as a source?

What are the values of **o1** and **o2** after the following expressions are evaluated?

(setf strm-out (make-string-output-stream))

(format strm-out "Hello~%")

(setf o1 (get-output-stream-string strm-out))

(format strm-out "Another hello~%")

(format strm-out "Goodbye~%")

(setf o2 (get-output-stream-string strm-out))

The second parameter to **format**, if not **nil**, must specify an output stream. If **nil** is used, what output stream is used? What does it mean to describe an output stream as a destination?

Enter the following.

> (describe *query-io*)

> (streamp *query-io*)

> (type-of *query-io*)

LESSON 14

```
>   (y-or-n-p)                              ; y-or-n-p uses the stream *query-io*
                                            ; Some sort of prompt should appear here.
                                            ; Enter y.

>   (y-or-n-p)                              ; Enter n after the prompt.

>   (y-or-n-p)                              ; Enter yes after the prompt.

>   (y-or-n-p)                              ; Enter N.

>   (y-or-n-p)                              ; Try y-or-p with numbers, words,
                                            ; (e.g., yes, no), and so on.

>   (y-or-n-p)

>   (y-or-n-p)

>   (y-or-n-p "Do you need help?")          ; Enter a Y.

>   (type-of (y-or-n-p))                    ; Enter a response.

>   (type-of (y-or-n-p))                    ; Enter an N.

>   (defun y-n()                            ; This is more
        (if (y-or-n-p "Continue?") (y-n))   ; convenient for
    )                                       ; exploring
                                            ; y-or-n-p.

>   (y-n)                                   ; Try a variety of responses here.
                                            ; Use y-n repeatedly.

>   (yes-or-no-p)                           ; Some sort of prompt should appear.
                                            ; Enter Y, and so on.
```

Characterize those responses for which **y-or-n-p** returns **t** and those for which it returns **nil**.

Complete the exploration of **yes-or-no-p** in a manner analogous to that for **y-or-n-p**. (**Yes-or-no-p** will also take a string parameter.) How do **yes-or-no-p** and **y-or-n-p** differ?

SUMMARY

Standard-input, ***Standard-output*** and ***query-io*** are predefined streams for input and output. **Read** may use an input stream and **format** may use an output stream.

Streamp, **input-stream-p** and **output-stream-p** are predicates for testing for streams.

Make-synonym-stream allows a stream to be renamed.

Functions like **make-string-input-stream**, **make-string-output-stream** and **get-output-stream-string** make it possible to use strings as streams.

Close terminates the input or output operations with a stream.

Format has a variety of options (using ~d and ~f) for the output of numbers.

Y-or-no-p and **yes-or-no-p** simplify and standardize queries.

LESSON 15
Files

```
;; ** Note: This lesson is implementation dependent.
```

Enter the following.

> (setq L '(a b c (d e f) g h i))

> (setq S "This a string.")

> (setq S2 "This is a string over two lines.")

> L

> S

> S2

> (princ L)

> (write L)

> (print L)

> (prin1 L)

> (pprint L)   ; Pretty PRINT

> (write S)

> (princ S)

> (print S)

> (prin1 S)

> (pprint S)

> (defun o-c(x)   ; Output function Comparisons
      (terpri)
      (princ ""Write: "") (write x) (terpri)
      (terpri)
      (princ "Print: ") (print x) (terpri)
      (terpri)
      (princ "Prin1: ") (prin1 x)   (terpri)
      (terpri)
      (princ "Princ: ") (princ x)   (terpri)
      (terpri)
      (princ "PPrint: ")   (pprint x) (terpri)
      (terpri)
)

> (o-c L)

> (o-c S)

> (o-c S2)

> (o-c 'a)

> (o-c #\A)

> (o-c 99)

> (o-c 123.456789)

> (setf NL1 '(a (b c) d (e (f g))))   ; Nested List

> NL1

> (setf NL2
      '(((a b (c d)) (e f (g h (i j (k l m n))))))
)

> NL2

> (o-c NL1)

LESSON 15

> (o-c NL2)

> *print-level*

> (setf *print-level* 2)

> (o-c L)

> (o-c NL1)

> (o-c NL2)

> (setf *print-level* 4)

> (o-c L)

> (o-c NL1)

> (o-c NL2)

Describe the differences of **write**, **princ**, **print**, **prin1**, and **pprint**. (It may be helpful to use **o-c** in doing this.)

What does *print-level* control?

Enter the following.
;; ** The strings "data.1", "data.2", and so on represent
;; ** legal file names for the operating system being
;; ** used. It may be necessary to change these for
;; ** the operating system actually used.

> (with-open-file (stream "data.1" :direction :output)
    (dotimes (i 10) (write i stream))
)

Exit Lisp and use the appropriate operating system command to examine the contents of data.1. Return to Lisp and enter the following.

> (with-open-file (stream "data.2" :direction :output)
     (dotimes (i 10) (print i stream))
)

Exit Lisp and use the appropriate operating system command to examine the contents of data.2. Return to Lisp and enter the following.

> (with-open-file (strm "data.3" :direction :output)
     (dotimes (i 10) (prin1 i strm)))

Exit Lisp and use the appropriate operating system command to examine the contents of data.3. Return to Lisp and enter the following.

> (with-open-file (strm "data.4" :direction :output)
     (dotimes (i 10) (princ i strm)))

Exit Lisp and use the appropriate operating system command to examine the contents of data.4. Return to Lisp and enter the following.

> (defun create-num-file (n fname)
     (with-open-file (strm fname :direction :output)
        (dotimes (i n) (print i strm))
)
)

> (create-num-file 20 "data.5")

Exit Lisp and use the appropriate operating system command to examine the contents of data.5. Return to Lisp and enter the following.

> (create-num-file 5 "data.5")

Exit Lisp and use the appropriate operating system command to examine the contents of data.5. Return to Lisp and enter the following.

> (with-open-file (strm "data.5")
     (loop
        (if (print (read strm)) (terpri) (return))
)
)

LESSON 15

```
> (with-open-file (strm "data.5")
      (loop
          (if (write (read strm)) (terpri) (return))
      )
  )

> (defun read-file (fname)
      (with-open-file (strm fname)
          (loop
              (if (write (read strm)) (terpri) (return))
          )
      )
  )

> (read-file "data.1")

> (dotimes (i 5)
      (read-file (format nil "data.~a" (+ i 1)))
      (terpri) (terpri)
  )

> (with-open-file (strm "data.5") (princ (boundp strm)))

> (boundp strm)

> (setq s (open "data.5"))

> (read s)

> (read s)

> (read s)

> (close s)

> (read s)

> (setq s (open "data.5" :if-does-not-exist nil))

> s

> (read s)

> (read s)

> (close s)

> (setq s (open "nogood.dat"))

> (setq s (open "nogood.dat" :if-does-not-exist nil))
```

> s

> (read s)

> (defun read-2 (fname)
       (when
           (with-open-file
               (strm fname :if-does-not-exist nil)
)
           (loop (if (write (read strm)) (terpri) (return)))
           (close strm)
)
)

> (read-2 "data.5")

> (read-2 "nogood.dat")

What is the effect upon **stream** and **"file"** of **(with-open-file (stream "file" ...)**?

Is **strm** bound to a file after the evaluation of **(with-open-file (strm "file name") ...)**?

Would **read** be possible with **strm** within the expression **(with-open-file (strm "file name" :direction :output)...)**

What is the default **:direction** of **with-open-file**?

Write a function with three arguments, each the name of a file. The first name is the name of an input file and the second two names are for output files. The function is to put all the numbers in the input file in one output file and everything else from the input file in the other output file.

LESSON 15

Enter the following. Again, file names may need to be changed to conform to the operating system being used.

```
> (with-open-file (strm "data.1" :direction :output)
      (dolist (x '(a b c (d e f) 1 2 3))
          (format strm "~a~%" x)
      )
  )

> (with-open-file (strm "data.1" :direction :input)
      (loop
          (if (null (princ (read strm))) (return) (terpri))
      )
  )

> (with-open-file (strm "data.1" :direction :input)
      (loop
          (princ (read strm (return) 'done))
          (terpri)
      )
  )

> (with-open-file (s "data.1" :direction :input)
      (loop
          (if (null (princ (read s nil))) (return) (terpri))
      )
  )

> (with-open-file (s "data.1" :direction :input)
      (loop
          (if (eql (princ (read s nil 'done)) 'done)
              (return)
              (terpri)
          )
      )
  )

> (with-open-file (s "data.1" :direction :input)
      (loop
          (if (eql (princ (read s nil 'done)) 'done)
             (return 'finished)
             (terpri)
          )
      )
  )
```

> (with-open-file (s "data.1" :direction :io)
        (loop
            (if (null (princ (read s nil nil))) (return) (terpri))
            (format s "~a~%" 123)
)
)

> (defun simple-reader (f)
        (with-open-file (s f)
            (loop
                (if (null (print (read s nil))) (return))
)
)
)

> (simple-reader "data.1")

> (setf strm2 (open "data.2" :direction :output))

> (format strm2 "~a" '(a b c))

> (format strm2 "~a" 123)

> (format strm2 "~a" 'thingamajig)

> (format strm2 "~a" "A string!")

> (close strm2)

> (simple-reader "data.2")

> (setf strm (open "data.2"))

> (read strm)

> (read strm)

> (read strm)

> (read strm)

> (close strm)

> (read strm)

> (simple-reader "data.2")

LESSON 15

> (setf strm (open "data.2" :direction :io))
> (file-length strm)
> (file-position strm)
> (format strm "~a~%" '(x y z))
> (file-position strm)
> (read strm)
> (file-position strm)
> (read strm)
> (file-position strm)
> (format strm "~a~%" 'a-symbol)
> (file-position strm)
> (format strm "~a~%" 'another-symbol)
> (setq L '(a b c d e f))
> (format strm "~a~%" L)
> (princ L strm)
> (princ L strm)
> (file-position strm 0)
> (read strm)
> (file-position strm 4)
> (read strm)
> (file-position strm :start)
> (read strm)
> (file-position strm :end)
> (read strm)
> (close strm)

> (simple-reader "data.2")

> (defun make-file (f)
      (with-open-file (strm f :direction :output)
         (loop
            (princ "-> ")
            (setq x (read))
            (if (null x) (return) (print x strm))
)
)
)

> (make-file "data.3")   ; Enter any objects here.
                                          ; End with nil.

> (simple-reader "data.3")

The elements of a file are considered to be numbered. What is the number of the first?

The function **read** may have up to three arguments. The first is the input stream. The second two arguments are for controlling what happens at the end of file. Describe their purpose.

There are two different ways of using **file-position: (file-position some-file-stream)** and **(file-position some-file-stream some-number)**. Describe how each of these work.

If the first argument of **format** is not **nil**, what does it denote?

SUMMARY

Write, **princ**, **print**, **prin1**, **pprint** are Lisp output functions, sending output to a stream which is usually associated with a file.

print-level controls the depth of printing of nested lists.

With-open-file and **open** are used to associate a stream with a file. **:direction** (**:input**, **:output** and **:io**) specifies the how the stream is to be used (as a source, a sink or both).

File-length gives the number of objects in a file. **File-position** can be used either to find the current position within a file or to specify the current position within a file.

LESSON 16
Association and Property Lists

Enter the following.

> (symbol-plist 'x)   ; PLIST for Property LIST

> (symbol-plist x)

> (setq x 10)

> (symbol-plist 'x)

> (get 'x 'num-val)

> (setf (get 'x 'num-val) 10)   ; SetF, not setQ,
                                       ; MUST be used here.

> (get 'x 'num-val)

> (symbol-plist 'x)

> (setf (get 'x 'letter-pos) 24)

> (symbol-plist 'x)

> (get 'x 'letter-pos)

LESSON 16

> (setf (get 'x 'letter-pos) 23)

> (symbol-plist 'x)

> (get 'x 'binary)

> (setf (get 'x 'binary) #b1010)

> (symbol-plist 'x)

> (remprop 'x 'binary)

> (symbol-plist 'x)

> (get 'x 'binary)

> (setf (get 'x 'name) nil)

> (symbol-plist 'x)

> (get 'x 'name)

> (get 'x 'last-name)

> (setf (get 'me 'name) 'jack)

> (setf (get 'me 'children) '(george ann))

> (get 'me 'children)

> (setf (get 'me 'children)
        (cons 'mary (get 'me 'children))
)

> (symbol-plist 'me)

> (setf (get 'me 'wife) 'sue)

> (symbol-plist 'me)

> (defun addprop(object property value)
        (setf (get object property) value)
)

> (addprop 'me 'dog 'spot)

> (symbol-plist 'me)

Suppose the following expressions are evaluated by the Lisp interpreter.

(setf (get 'friend 'name) 'helen)

(setf (get 'friend 'phone) '784-1234)

(setf (get 'friend 'address) '(123 oak-street))

(setf (get 'friend 'pets) nil)

(remprop 'friend 'phone)

What is returned by each of the following?

(symbol-plist 'friend)

(get 'friend 'name)

(get 'friend 'pets)

(get 'friend 'dog)

(get 'friend 'phone)

Write a sequence of statements that records, using a plist, the name, address, and age of a person.

Write a function which increases the age recorded in the plist that was generated by the preceding statements.

Write a function which deletes all the properties of an object which are **nil**.

LESSON 16

Enter the following.

> (eql 'a 'a)
> (equal 'a 'a)
> (eql 'a ')
> (equal 'a 'b)
> (eql (cons 'a nil) (cons 'a nil))
> (equal (cons 'a nil) (cons 'a nil))
> (setq L '(a b c))
> (setq LL '(a b c))
> (eql L LL)
> (equal L LL)
> (eql L '(a b c))
> (equal L '(a b c))
> (eql L (cons 'a (car L)))
> (equal L (cons 'a (car L)))
> (eql L (cons (car L) (cdr L)))
> (equal L (cons (car L) (cdr L)))

What is the difference between **eql** and **equal**?

When should **equal** (and not **eql**) be used?

Enter the following.

> '(x . y)   ; This is called a dotted list or
>   ; dotted pair.

> (cons 'x 'y)

> (cons 1 2)

> (cons "X" "Y")

> (cons '(x y) 'z)

> (cons 'x '(y . z))

> '(y . nil)

> (car '(x . y))

> (cdr '(x . y))

> (cdr '(x y))

> (equal (cons 'x 'y) '(x . y))

> (equal '(x . nil) '(x))

> (equal '(x y z) '(x y z . nil))

> (equal (cons 'x nil) '(x))

> (append '(a b) '(x y))

> (append 'a 'x)

> (append '(a b) 'z)

> (append '(a b) 'x 'y)

LESSON 16   185

> (append '(a b) '(x y) 'z)

> '(x . (y))

> '(x . (y . z))

> '(x . (y z))

> '(x (y . z))

> '(x y . (a b))

> (listp '(x . y))

> (listp (cons 'x 'y))

> (consp '(x . y))

> (consp '(x y))

> (consp '(x))

> (consp nil)

> (listp nil)

What are the values of the following expressions?

(cons 4 5)

(cons 'a '(b c))

(cons '(a b) 'c)

'(a . nil)

(cons 'a nil)

(equal (cons 'a nil) '(a . nil))

(equal '(a) '(a . nil))

(consp 'a)

(consp '(a))

(consp '(x y z))

(consp '(x . y))

(consp (cons 'x 'y))

(consp (cdr '(x . y)))

(consp (cdr '(x y)))

There is one value for which **listp** and **consp** do not agree. What is it?

Enter the following.

> (setf as-list nil)   ; AS-LIST for ASsociation LIST
>   ; or A-LIST

> as-list

> (acons 'one 1 as-list)

> as-list

> (setf as-list (acons 'one 1 as-list))

> as-list

> (setf as-list (acons 'two 2 as-list))

> (setf as-list (acons 'three 3 as-list))

> as-list

> (assoc 'two as-list)

> (assoc 'one as-list)

> (assoc 'four as-list)

> (setf as-list (acons 'four (+ 1 3) as-list))

> as-list

LESSON 16

```
> (assoc 'four as-list)
> (setf as-list (acons 'three 'iii as-list))
> (assoc 'three as-list)
> (setf as-list (acons 'two 'ii as-list))
> as-list
> (assoc 'two as-list)
> (assoc 'four as-list)
> (rassoc 1 as-list)
> (rassoc 'iii as-list)
> (rassoc 3 as-list)
> (rassoc 'four as-list)
> (rassoc 5 as-list)
> (setf as-list (acons 'trois 3 as-list))
> (rassoc 3 as-list)
> (assoc 'zero as-list)
> (setf as-list (acons 'zero nil as-list))
> (setf as-list (cons '(five . 5) as-list))
> (assoc 'five as-list)
> (rassoc 5 as-list)
> (setf as-list (cons (cons 'six 6) as-list))
> (assoc 'six as-list)
> (rassoc 6 as-list)
> (setf as-list (cons '(seven 7) as-list))
> (assoc 'seven as-list)
> (rassoc 7 as-list)
```

Suppose the following are entered.

(setf thing nil)

(setf thing (acons 'shape 'square thing))

(setf thing (acons 'x-coord 8
  (acons 'y-coord 4 thing))
)

(setf thing (acons 'color 'red thing))

(setf thing (acons 'area 4 thing))

What is returned by the following?

thing

(assoc 'color thing)

(assoc 'z-coord thing)

(assoc 'side thing)

(rassoc 'red thing)

(rassoc 4 thing)

It should be evident from the preceding that an association list is a list of dotted pairs. Write a function, **assocp**, which returns **t** if the argument is in the form of an association list (or **nil**) and **nil** if the argument is not. (Hint: write a function **pairp** which tests whether an object is a pair.)

Enter the following.

> (setf L '(a b c d e))

> L

LESSON 16

> (rplaca L 1)

> L

> (rplacd L 'z)

> L

> (rplacd L '(b c d e))

> L

> (rplaca (cddr L) 2)

> L

> (rplacd (cdddr L) '(d e f))

> L

> (rplacd (cddr L) '(d e))

> L

> (setf LL '((a b) (c d) (e g)))

> LL

> (rplaca (car LL) 1)

> LL

> (rplacd (car LL) 2)

> LL

> (rplacd (car LL) '(2))

> LL

> (rplaca LL '(a b))

> LL

> (rplaca (cadr LL) 3)

> LL

> (rplacd (cadr LL) 4)

> LL

> (rplacd (cadr LL) '(4))

> (rplaca (cdr LL) '(c d))

> LL

> (rplaca (cddr LL) '(5 6))

> LL

> (rplaca (caddr LL) 'e)

> LL

> (rplacd (caddr LL) 'f)

> LL

> (rplacd (caddr LL) '(f))

> LL

> (setf as-list '((one . 1) (two . 2)))

> (assoc 'one as-list)

> (assoc 'two as-list)

> (rassoc 2 as-list)

> (setf as-list
     (acons 'three 3 (acons 'four 4 as-list))
)

> (assoc 'four as-list)

> (rplacd (assoc 'four as-list) 'iv)

> as-list

> (assoc 'four as-list)

> (rplaca (assoc 'three as-list) 'trois)

> as-list

> (assoc 'trois as-list)

> (rassoc 3 as-list)

> (rassoc 4 as-list)

What is the value of **L** after each of the following expressions are evaluatated?

(setq L '(1 2 3 4))

(rplaca L 100)

(rplacd L '(200 300))

(rplaca (cdr L) 500)

Give the value of **alphalist** after each of the following is evaluated.

(setf alphalist
  '((Alpha . A) (Beta . B) (Epsilon . E))
)

(rplaca (car alphalist) 'biga)

(rplacd (car alphalist) 'aa)

(rplaca (cadr alphalist) 'beth)

(rplacd (cadr alphalist) 'bb)

(rplaca (cdr alphalist) 'x)

Suppose **L** is bound to the list **(a b c d e f)**. Write a Lisp expression which replaces the **c** in the list with **ccc**.

Write a function which replaces the nth object in a list with a specified object. (The objects in the list are numbered starting with **0**.) That is, if the function's name is **replacen**, **replacen(L n x)** replaces the nth object in the list **L** with **x**. (The value the function returns is unimportant.) For example,

```
> (setq letters '(a b c d e f g))
(A B C D E F G)
> (replacen letters 3 'delta)
(DELTA E F G)                      ; This value doesn't matter.
> letters
(A B C DELTA E F G)                ; Note where DELTA appears.
> (replacen letters 5 'phi)
(PHI G)
> letters
(A B C DELTA E PHI G)
```

SUMMARY

Each symbol has a property list or plist which contains data for the symbol. **Symbol-plist** returns this list. **Get** is used to manipulate parts of a plist. **Remprop** deletes a property from a plist.

Lists are built from dotted pairs, technically known as **conses** or **cons** cells. **Consp** is a predicate testing whether an object is a **cons**. The first part of a **cons** is its **car**, the second is its **cdr**.

Eql tests whether two objects are the same. **Equal** tests whether the contents of dotted pairs are the same.

An association list or a-list is a list of dotted pairs. **Acons** is used to add to an a-list. **Assoc** searches an a-list for a dotted pair with a specified **car**. **Rassoc** searches an a-list for a dotted pair with a specified **cdr**.

LESSON 17
Equality

Enter the following.

> (eq 7 7)

> (eq 7 8)

> (eql 7 7)

> (eql 7 8)

> (equal 7 7)

> (equal 7 8)

> (equalp 7 7)

> (equalp 7 8)
```
;; ** In the following, each of the lines within quotations
;; ** (except the last) ends with ~%~<RET>. The
;; ** return must immediately follow the last tilde.
```

> (defun equal-test (x y)   ; Compare equality
    (format nil   ; predicates
       "Objects: ~a   ~a ~%~

```
            Predicate       Result    ~%~
            eq              ~a        ~%~
            eql             ~a        ~%~
            equal           ~a        ~%~
            equalp          ~a        ~%"
         x y (eq x y) (eql x y) (equal x y) (equalp x y)
    )
  )
```

> (equal-test 7 7)

> (equal-test 7 8)

> (equal-test 9876543210 9876543210)

> (equal-test 3 3.0)

> (equal-test 3 9/3)

> (equal-test 0.5 1/2)

> (equal-test 1.0e2 100)

> (equal-test 0.05 5e-2)

> (equal-test 7 (+ 3 4))

> (equal-test 'a 'a)

> (equal-test 'a 'A)

> (equal-test 'a 'b)

> (equal-test 'a #\a)

> (equal-test 'a #\A)

> (equal-test a a)

> (setf a 8)

> (equal-test a 8)

> (equal-test 'a 8)

> (setf b 8)

> (equal-test a b)

LESSON 17

> (equal-test (* 2 a) 16)

> (equal-test nil nil)

> (equal-test t t)

> (equal-test t nil)

> (equal-test 't t)

> (equal-test 'nil nil)

> (equal-test nil ())

> (setf N nil)

> (equal-test N nil)

> (equal-test '(a b c) '(a b c))

> (equal-test '(a b c) '(x y z))

> (equal-test '(a b (c d)) '(a b (c d)))

> (equal-test 'a '(a b c))

> (equal-test (cons 'a 'b)) (cons 'a 'b)))

> (setf L1 '(a b c))

> (setf L2 '(a b c))

> (setf L3 L1)

> (equal-test L1 L1)

> (equal-test L1 L2)

> (equal-test L1 L3)

> (equal-test (car L1) (car L1))

> (equal-test (cdr L1) (cdr L1))

> (equal-test (car L1) (car L2))

> (equal-test (cdr L1) (cdr L2))

> (equal-test (car L1) (car L3))

> (equal-test (cdr L1) (cdr L3))

> (equal-test (cons 'a (cdr L1)) L1)

> (equal-test nil (cdr L1))

> (equal-test nil (cddr L1))

> (equal-test nil (cdddr L1))

> (equal-test #\A #\A)

> (equal-test #\A #\B)

> (equal-test #\A #\a)

> (equal-test "Hello" "Hello")

> (equal-test "Hello" "Goodbye")

> (equal-test "Hello " "Hello")

> (equal-test "Hello" "HELLO")

> (equal-test #\A "A")

The four equality predicates, **eq**, **eql**, **equal**, and **equalp**, do not measure equality in quite the same way. Which predicate is strictest or least general (i.e., gives **nil** for the most comparisons)? Which predicate is the least strict or most general?

Why do you think Common Lisp has four different (general purpose) predicates for testing equality?

Enter the following.

LESSON 17

> (= 2 3)

> (= 2 2)

> (= 2 2.0)

> (= 'a 'a)

> (char= #\a #\a)

> (char= #\a #\b)

> (char= #\a #\A)

> (char-equal #\a #\a)

> (char-equal #\a #\b)

> (char-equal #\a #\A)

> (string= "up" "up")

> (string= "up" "down")

> (string= "up" "UP")

> (string-equal "up" "up")

> (string-equal "up" "down")

> (string-equal "up" "UP")

The predicates =, **char=**, **char-equal**, **string=**, and **string-equal** are equality predicates suitable for particular types of objects. What are the types for each?

Which is more general (not **nil** in more cases), **char=** or **char-equal**?

Which is more general (not **nil** in more cases), **string=** or **string-equal**?

Compare the five predicates =, **char=**, **char-equal**, **string=**, and **string-equal** to **eq, eql, equal** and **equalp**. For example, = is most like which of **eq, eql, equal,** and **equalp** restricted to numbers?

SUMMARY

Lisp has four general purpose equality predicates: **eq**, **eql**, **equal**, and **equalp**.

Special purpose equality predicates are = (for numbers), **char=** and **char-equal** (for characters), and **string=** and **string-equal** (for strings).

LESSON 18
Characters and Strings

```
;; ** To a certain extent the results of this lesson
;; ** are implementation dependent.
```

Enter the following.

> (char-int #\A)

> (code-char 65)

> (code-char #x41)

> (code-char #o101)

> (code-char 7)

> (code-char 26)

> (princ #\A)

> (princ (format nil "~a ~a" #\B #\b))

> (princ #\space)

> (princ (format nil "¦~a¦" #\space))   ; The ¦ symbols
                                                ; are markers.

> (princ #\newline)

199

\> (princ (format nil "¡~a!" #\newline))

\> (defun char-table (n)
       (dotimes (i n)
           (setq c (code-char i))
           (princ
               (format nil
                   "~3d ~8a ~8s ~3a ~3a ~3a ~3a ~3a ~3a ~3a ~3a~%"
                   i c c
                   (standard-char-p c)
                   (graphic-char-p c)
                   (alpha-char-p c)
                   (alphanumericp c)
                   (upper-case-p c)
                   (lower-case-p c)
                   (both-case-p c)
                   (digit-char-p c)
)
)
)
)

\> (char-table 128)

\> char-code-limit   ; a constant, so no parentheses

\> (char-table char-code-limit)

\> (char< #\a #\c)

\> (char< #\c #\a)

\> (char< #\a #\e #\i #\o #\u)

\> (char< #\a #\e #\i #\u #\o)

\> (char< #\a #\b #\b)

\> (char<= #\a #\b #\b)

\> (defun char-comp (c1 c2)
       (princ
           (format nil "char=   ~a ~a ~a~%" c1 c2
               (char= c1 c2)
)
)
       (princ
           (format nil "char/= ~a ~a ~a~%" c1 c2
               (char/= c1 c2)

LESSON 18

```
              )
          )
          (princ
              (format nil "char<     ~a ~a ~a~%" c1 c2
                  (char< c1 c2)
              )
          )
          (princ
              (format nil "char>     ~a ~a ~a~%" c1 c2
                  (char> c1 c2)
              )
          )
          (princ
              (format nil "char<= ~a ~a ~a~%" c1 c2
                  (char<= c1 c2)
              )
          )
          (princ
              (format nil "char>= ~a ~a ~a~%" c1 c2
                  (char>= c1 c2)
              )
          )
          (terpri)
      )
> (char-comp #\a #\A)

> (char-comp #\a #\a)

> (char-comp #\A #\0)

> (char-comp #\a #\0)

> (char-comp #\A #\9)

> (char-comp #\a #\9)

> (char-comp #\0 #\2)

> (char-comp #\Z #\a)

> (char-comp #\z #\A)

> (setq bb #\B b #\b c #\c)

> (char-comp bb b)

> (char-comp b c)
```

> (char-equal #\A #\A)

> (char-equal #\A #\a)

> (char-equal #\A #\B)

> (char-equal bb b)

> (char-equal b c)

> (char-equal #\A #\a #\a)

> (char-equal #\A #\A #\B)

> (char-not-equal bb b)

> (char-not-equal b c)

> (char-lessp bb b)

> (char-lessp b c)

> (char-lessp bb b c)

> (char-greaterp bb b)

> (char-greaterp b c)

> (char-not-greaterp bb b)

> (char-not-greater b c)

> (char-not-lessp bb b)

> (char-not-lessp b c)

> (char-upcase #\a)

> (char-upcase #\A)

> (char-downcase #\a)

> (char-downcase #\A)

> (character 'x)   ; Character is a "coercion" function.

> (setq yy 'y)

> (character yy)

> (character 7)

What are the values of the following expressions?

(char= #\a #\a #\a)

(char= #\a #\b #\a)

(char> #\z #\y #\x)

(char> #\0 #\9 #\8)

(char>= #\9 #\9 #\8)

(char>= #\9 #\8 #\9)

(char-equal #\d #\D)

(char-equal #\e #\d)

Compare the characters produced by **(char-table 128)** with the ASCII character set. Are there any differences? If there are differences, compare with another character set (e.g., EBCDIC).

Enter the following.

> (setq st1 "abcdefghijkl")

> (setq st2 "abcd abcd")

> (char st1 0)

> (char st2 4)

> (string= st1 st2)

> (string= st1 st2 :end1 4 :end2 4)

> (string= st1 st2 :end1 5 :end2 5)

> (string= st1 st2 :end1 4 :start2 5 :end2 9)

> (string= st1 st2 :start1 2 :end1 4 :end2 2)

> (string= st1 st2 :start1 2 :end1 4 :start2 2 :end2 4)

> (string= st1 st2 :start1 2 :end1 4 :start2 7 :end2 9)

> (string= st1 st2 :end2 3 :end1 3)

> (string< "cat" "dog")

> (string< "dog" "cat")

> (string< "CAT" "dog")

> (string< "cat" "DOG")

> (string< "cat" "cat")

> (string<= "cat" "cat")

> (string<= "CAT" "cat")

> (string<= "cat" "CAT")

> (string-equal "cat" "cat")

> (string-equal "cat" "CAT")

> (string-equal "cat" "dog")

> (string-not-equal "cat" "cat")

> (string-not-equal "cat" "CAT")

> (string-not-equal "cat" "dog")

> (string-lessp "dog" "cat")

> (string-lessp "DOG" "cat")

> (string-greaterp "cat" "CAT")

> (string-greaterp "cat" "dog")

> (string-greaterp "CAT" "dog")

LESSON 18

> (string-not-greaterp "cat" "CAT")

> (string-not-greaterp "cat" "dog")

> (string-not-greaterp "CAT" "dog")

> (string-not-lessp "cat" "CAT")

> (string-not-lessp "cat" "dog")

> (string-not-lessp "CAT" "dog")

> (make-string 5 :initial-element #\s)

> (make-string 5 :initial-element #\space)

> (make-string 5)   ; No initial-element given,
                                            ; use default.

> (string-trim '(#\space) "   aaaaaa   ")

> (string-trim '(#\- #\+) "---a+a+a---a+++")

> (string-left-trim '(#\space) "   a a a a   ")

> (string-right-trim '(#\space) "   a a a a   ")

> (setq s "How are you today?")

> (string-upcase s)

> (string-upcase s :start 4 :end 9)

> (string-downcase s)

> (string-capitalize s)

> (string-capitalize s :start 8)

> (string-capitalize "HOW are You tODAY?")

> (string 'abc)   ; String is a coercion function.

> (string #\a)

> (string 123)

> (setq !a b c! 123)

> '|a b c|

> |a b c|

> (princ '|a b c|)

> (string '|a b c|)

What are the values of the following?

(string= "ABC" "abc")

(string-equal "ABC" "abc")

(string= "AB CD" "ABCD")

(string= "AB CD" "ABCD" :start1 0 :end1 1
                      :start2 0 :end2 1)

Write a function which compares two strings for equality. The function is to ignore leading and trailing blank spaces and not to distinguish between upper and lower case letters. Any non-**nil** value may be returned if the strings are equal in this sense. For example, if the function is named **str-eql**,

(str-eql " DOG " "dog") => 3

(str-eql "cat" " dog ") => **nil**

Note: The functions that follow may also be used with objects other than strings. Enter the following.

> (setq st "abcdefghijklmnop")

> (length st)

> (reverse st)

> (subseq st 3)

LESSON 18

> (subseq st 0)
> (subseq st 1)
> (subseq st 2 4)
> (subseq st 2 99)
> (subseq st 99)
> (elt st 2)
> (elt st 5)
> (concatenate 'string st "ABC")
> (remove #\a st)
> (remove #\f st)
> (delete #\p st)
> st
> (substitute #\z #\a st)
> st
> (setq st "ababababcdefghijxyxyxyxy")
> (position #\a st)
> (position #\c st)
> (position #\A st)
> (count #\a st)
> (count #\c st)
> (count #\z st)
> (find #\b st)
> (find #\z st)
> st
> (sort st 'char<)

> (sort st 'char>)

What are the values of the following?

(length "A B C")

(reverse "ABC")

(subseq "A B C D" 2 4)

(reverse (subseq "A B C D E" 3 5))

(position #\C "A B C D E")

Write a function returns the number of words in a string. For the purposes of this exercise, a word is either at the beginning of the string or preceded by one or more blanks. For example,

(**word-count "cat and dog"**) => **3**

(**word-count " elephant "**) => **1**

SUMMARY

Common Lisp provides many functions for working with characters and strings.

Special characters are #**space** and #**newline**.

Characters are classified into many (overlapping) groups, each of which has a corresponding predicate (e.g., **standard-char-p**, **alpha-char-p**).

The functions **char-int**, **code-char** and **character** are conversion functions between characters and other types.

Comparison predicates for characters and strings begin with **char** and **string** and are followed by =, /=, ... or **-equal**, **-not-equal**, ... When the suffix is spelled, upper and lower case letters are considered the same.

Upper and lower case versions of characters and strings are returned by **char-upcase**, **string-downcase**, etc. For strings, keys may be used to specify the part of the string to be converted.

A variety of functions are provided for the manipulation of strings: **make-string, string-trim, string-left-trim, length, subseq, elt, sort, concatenate, substitute, remove, delete, reverse, position, count, find.** (Many apply to other sequences of objects, e.g. lists.)

LESSON 19
Numbers

Enter the following.

> (+ 1/2 2/3)

> (+ 1 1/2)

> (− 1/2)

> (− 2 1/2)

> (* 2/3 1/2)

> (* 3 5/6)

> (/ 12 4)

> (/ 12 5)

> (/ −3 6)

> (/ 3 −6)

> (/ 4 5 7)

> (/ 4 (/ 5 7)

LESSON 19

> (/ 4/5 2/3)
> (setq fifth 1/5 tenth 1/10)
> (+ fifth tenth)
> (* fifth tenth)
> (/ fifth tenth)
> (fifth '(a b c d e f))
> (numerator 3/5)
> (denominator 3/5)
> (numerator fifth)
> (denominator tenth)
> (numerator 6/9)
> (denominator 6/9)
> (numerator 2)
> (denominator 2)
> (integerp 8)
> (integerp −8)
> (integerp 0)
> (integerp 2/3)
> (integerp 6/3)
> (integerp 1.2)
> (rationalp 8)
> (rationalp −8)
> (rationalp 0)
> (rationalp 2/3)
> (rationalp 6/3)

> (rationalp 1.2)

> (oddp 2)

> (oddp −3)

> (evenp 4)

> (evenp −5)

What are the values of the following expressions?

(+ 3/4 2/3)

(+ 1/2 3/2)

(− 3/4)

(− 3 4)

(* 2/5 5/7)

(* 2 (+ 3/4 2/5))

(/ 2 3)

(/ 8 4)

(numerator 4/9)

(denominator 4/9)

(integerp 200)

(rationalp 200)

(integerp 22/7)

(rationalp 22/7)

Suppose **n** is has a value such that **(integerp n)** evaluates to **t**. What is the value of **(denominator n)**?

LESSON 19

If **n** is such that **(integerp (/ n 2))** is **t**, what is the value of **(evenp n)**?

    Enter the following.

> (+ 1 2.3)
> (+ 1.5 2/3)
> (+ 1.5 2.5)
> (+ 1/2 0.5)
> (+ 2 2.1 5/2)
> (− 1.2)
> (− 1.2 7.8)
> (* 2.1 3)
> (* 2.1 1.2)
> (* 4 0.5)
> (* 0.25 2 2.0)
> (/ 4 2)
> (/ 4 3)
> (/ 4.0 2.0)
> (/ 4.0 2)
> (/ 4 2.0)
> (/ 1/2 0.5)
> (floatp 8)
> (floatp −8)
> (floatp 0)

> (floatp 2/3)

> (floatp 6/3)

> (floatp 1.2)

> (setq x 1.2345e2)

> x

> (integerp x)

> (rationalp x)

> (floatp x)

> (+ x 1)

> (* 10000 x)

> (integerp (* 10000 x))

> (* x 0.00001)

> (setq y 1.2345-e2)

> y

> (floatp y)

> (+ x y)

> (* 10000 y)

> (plusp 2.0)

> (minusp 2.0)

> (defun plus-minus (n)
    (princ
        (format nil "~a   plusp: ~a   minusp: ~a"
            n (plusp n) (minusp n))
)
)
    (terpri)
)

> (plus-minus 3.3)

LESSON 19

> (plus-minus −4.5)

> (plus-minus 2/3)

> (plus-minus −5/4)

> (plus-minus 9.87654e3)

> (plus-minus 9.87654e-3)

> (plus-minus −9.87654e3)

> (plus-minus −9.87654e-3)

> (plus-minus 0)

> (plus-minus 0.0)

> (plus-minus −0.0)

> pi

> (integerp pi)

> (floatp pi)

> (cos pi)

> (sin pi)

> (integerp (/ pi pi))

> (setq pi-over-2 (/ pi 2))

> (cos pi-over-2)

> (sin pi-over-2)

> (abs 2)

> (abs −2)

> (abs 3/4)

> (abs −3/4)

> (abs 1.2)

> (abs −1.2)

> (abs 0)

> (sqrt 9)

> (sqrt 9.0)

> (sqrt 1/4)

> (sqrt 0.25)

> (sqrt −9)

What are the values of the following?

(+ 1.2 0.3)

(* 1/2 4.4)

(integerp 0.2)

(rationalp 0.2)

(floatp 0.2)

(plusp (− 2.3 3.4))

(minusp 6.66666e-6)

(integerp 2.1212e2)

(rationalp 2.1212e2)

(floatp 2.1212e2)

(abs 2.35e-4)

(abs −2.35e4)

(cos 0)

(sin 0)

If **(numberp n)** is t, is **(plusp (abs n))** also t?

LESSON 19

If **(integerp n)** is **t**, is **(rationalp n)**? What about **(floatp n)**?

Enter the following.

> `(= 2 2)`

> `(= 2 3)`

> `(= −4 −4)`

> `(= 2 2.0)`

> `(= 2 4/2)`

> `(= 0.25 1/4)`

> `(= 0.1 1/10)`

> `(= 0.01 1e-2)`

> `(= 3)`

> `(= 3 3 3 3 3 3)`

> `(= 3 4 3 3 3 3)`

> `(= 3 3 3 3 3 4)`

> `(= 3 9/3 3.0e0 (/ 12.0 4.0) 0.03e2 300e-2)`

> `(/= 2)`

> `(/= 2 4)`

> `(/= 2 2)`

> `(/= 2 2 4)`

> `(/= 2 3 4)`

> `(< 2)`

> (< 2 4)

> (< 4 2)

> (< 2 2)

> (< 2 2 4)

> (< 2 3 4)

> (< 2 4 8 16 32)

> (< 2 8 4 16 32)

> (<= 7)

> (<= 7 8)

> (<= 8 7)

> (<= 7 7)

> (<= 1 3 3 5 7 7 9)

> (> 5)

> (> 5 6)

> (> 6 5)

> (> 6 5 4)

> (> 6 5 5)

> (>= 5)

> (>= 5 6)

> (> 6 5)

> (>= 6 5 4)

> (>= 6 5 5)

What are the values of the following?

(= 10 20/2 (/ 4e2 40))

LESSON 19

(< 2 4 5 6 6 8)

(<= 2 4 5 6 6 8)

(/= 2 3 4 2)

What integer values for **n** make the expression (< **3 n 8**) have the value **t**?

What integer values for **n** make the expression (<= **4 n 6**) have the value **t**?

Enter the following.

> (setq x 3.4)
> (floor x)
> (ceiling x)
> (truncate x)
> (round x)
> (setq x 3.7)
> (floor x)
> (ceiling x)
> (truncate x)
> (round x)
> (setq x −3.2)
> (floor x)
> (ceiling x)
> (truncate x)

> (round x)

> (setq x −3.8)

> (floor x)

> (ceiling x)

> (truncate x)

> (round x)

> (setq x 7/3)

> (floor x)

> (ceiling x)

> (truncate x)

> (round x)

> (float 7)

> (float 1/2)

> (float 2/3)

> (rational 1.2)

> (rational 2.0)

> (rational 0.111111)

> (rational (float 1/3))

> (float (rational 0.09090909))

The functions **floor, ceiling, round, truncate,** and **rational** are coercion functions; they coerce one type of number to be another. For each of these functions state the type of number that is returned.

LESSON 19

Enter the following.

> (exp 1)
> (exp 2)
> (exp 0)
> (exp −1)
> (exp 1/2)
> (exp 0.3)
> (expt 2 3)
> (expt 3 2)
> (expt 2 −3)
> (expt −3 2)
> (expt 1/2 3)
> (expt 3 1/2)
> (expt 0.5 3)
> (expt 3 0.5)
> (log 2)
> (log 1)
> (log 3)
> (log (exp 1))
> (log (exp 2))
> (log 8 2)
> (log 16 2)
> (log 2 2)
> (log 1/2 2)

> (log 3 2)

> (log 9 3)

> (log 3 3)

> (log 2 3)

> (log 1 /27 3)

Write the following in the usual mathematical notation. (Assume all symbols represent numbers.)

(exp x)

(expt m n)

If **n** denotes a number, what is the value of **(log n n)**? (Assume no error occurs.)

If **x** and **n** denote numbers what is the value of **(expt n (log x n))**? (Assume no errors occur.)

Enter the following.

> (random 10)

> (random 100)

> (random 10.5)

> (defun rand-list (num bound)
     (dotimes (i num)
         (princ (random bound))
         (terpri)
)
)

LESSON 19

```
>   (rand-list 4 10)

>   (rand-list 20 100)

>   (rand-list 20 (float 100))

>   (setq x 10)

>   x

>   (incf x)

>   x

>   (incf x)

>   x

>   (incf x 0.5)

>   x

>   (decf x)

>   x

>   (decf x 0.5)

>   x
```

Write a function of two arguments, both integers, which returns a random integer between the two integers, inclusively. Check that the first number is less than the second. (If the first number exceeds the second, use the values in reverse order. If the two numbers are the same, the function returns their common value.) For example,

(random-between 3 88) => an integer at least 3 and no more than 88

(random-between 99 2) => an integer at least 2 and no more than 99

(random-between 23 23) => 23

(Note: If **n** is an integer, **(<= 0 (random n) (− n 1))** is t but **(< 0 (random n) n)** and **(< 1 (random n) n)** may not be.)

If **n** denotes a number, what are the values of the following?

(decf (incf n))

(incf n n)

SUMMARY

Common Lisp provides several numeric types with appropriate predicates: **integerp, rationalp,** and **floatp**. Other predicates test for properties of numbers (**plusp, minusp**) or integers (**oddp, evenp**).

Numerator and **denominator** return part of a fraction.

Coercion functions (**floor, ceiling, round, truncate,** and **rational**) convert between numbers of differing types.

Comparisons of numbers are done using $=$, $/=$, $<$, $<=$, $>$ and $>=$.

Common mathematical functions (**cos, sin, abs, sqrt, exp, expt, log**) are predefined as is the constant **pi**.

Random generates random integers.

Incf and **decf** return a number increased or decreased.

LESSON 20
Arrays

Enter the following.

> (setq v (make-array 7))

> (dotimes (i 7) (setf (aref v i) (* 10 i)))

> (aref v 0)

> (aref v 1)

> (aref v 2)

> (aref v 6)

> (aref v 7)

> (dotimes (i 7)
        (princ (format nil "~a   ~a~%" i (aref v i)))
)

> (setf (aref v 2) 'v-two)

> (aref v 2)

> (setf (aref v 0) nil)

> (aref v 0)

> (setf (aref v 3) "v Three ")

> (aref v 3)

> (dotimes (i 7)
        (princ (format nil "~a   ~a~%" i (aref v i)))
)

> (defun make-vec-one (vec veclen)
        (do (i veclen)
            (setf (aref vec i) 1)
)
)

> (make-vec-one (v 7))

> (dotimes (i 7)
        (princ (format nil "~a ~a~%" i (aref v i)))
)

> (setq m (make-array '(4 5)))

> (dotimes (i 4)
        (dotimes (j 5)
            (setf (aref m i j) (+ (* 100 i) j))
)
)

> (aref m 0 0)

> (aref m 0 1)

> (aref m 1 0)

> (aref m 1 1)

> (aref m 4 4)

> (aref m 3 4)

> (aref m 3 5)

> (defun print-matrix (mat dim0 dim1)
        (dotimes (i dim0)
            (dotimes (j dim1)
                (princ
                    (format nil "~a   ~a   ~a~%" i j (aref mat i j))

LESSON 20

```
            )
          )
        )
> (print-matrix m 4 5)
> (setf (aref m 0 0) "This is an array.")
> (aref m 0 0)
> (setf (aref m 1 2) '(m 1 2))
> (aref m 1 2)
> (car (aref m 1 2))
> (cdr (aref m 1 2))
> (setf (aref m 2 3) 'two-three)
> (aref m 2 3)
> (setf (aref m 3 4) "Three Four")
> (aref m 3 4)
> (+ (aref m 1 3) (aref m 3 1))
> (print-matrix m 4 5)
> (defun make-all-nums(a dim0 dim1)
      (dotimes (i dim0)
          (dotimes (j dim1)
              (if (not (numberp (aref a i j)))
                  (setf (aref a i j) 0)
              )
          )
      )
  )
> (make-all-nums m 4 5)
> (print-matrix m 4 5)
```

Suppose the following expressions are evaluated.

`(setq e1 (make-array 6))`

```
(let ((L ()))
  (dotimes (i 6)
    (setf (aref v i) (setq L (cons i L)))
  )
)
```

What are the values of the following expressions?

(aref e1 0)

(aref e1 1)

(car (aref e1 4))

What are the values of **n** that may be used in the expression **(aref e1 n)**?

Suppose the following expressions are evaluated.

(make-array e2 '(7 8))

```
(dotimes (i 7)
  (dotimes (i 8)
    (setf (aref e2 i j) (list i j))
  )
)
```

What are the values of the following?

(aref e2 3 4)

(aref e2 4 5)

(append (aref 0 1) (aref 2 3))

Comment upon what happens when an array is used as a function's argument and **aref** is used with the parameter. What can happen to values in the original array?

LESSON 20

Enter the following.

```
> (setq v (make-array 12))
> (arrayp v)
> (vectorp v)
> (setq x 10)
> (arrayp x)
> (vectorp x)
> (array-rank v)
> (array-dimensions v)
> (array-dimension v 0)       ; The preceding function ended
                              ; with s. This one doesn't.
> (array-total-size v)
> (array-in-bounds-p v 0)
> (array-in-bounds-p v 6)
> (array-in-bounds-p v 11)
> (array-in-bounds-p v 12)
> (array-in-bounds-p v 13)
> (setq m2 (make-array '(4 5)))
> (arrayp m2)
> (vectorp m2)
> (array-rank m2)
> (array-dimensions m2)
```

> (array-dimension m2 0)

> (array-dimensions m2 1)

> (array-total-size m2)

> (array-in-bounds-p m2 0 3)

> (array-in-bounds-p m2 2 3)

> (array-in-bounds-p m2 6 9)

> (array-in-bounds-p m2 4 5)

> (array-in-bounds-p m2 3 4)

> (array-in-bounds-p m2 4 3)

> (setq m3 (make-array '(6 8 10))

> (arrayp m3)

> (vectorp m3)

> (array-rank m3)

> (array-dimensions m3)

> (array-dimension m3 0)

> (array-dimension m3 1)

> (array-dimension m3 2)

> (array-total-size m3)

> (array-in-bounds-p m3 0 1 0)

> (array-in-bounds-p m3 2 3 4)

> (array-in-bounds-p m3 4 6 8)

> (array-in-bounds-p m3 4 5 10)

> array-rank-limit

> array-dimension-limit

> array-total-size-limit

LESSON 20

> (setq mm (make-array (+ 1 array-dimension-limit)))

Suppose the following expression is evaluated.

(setq e3 (make-array '(4 8)))

What are the values of the following?

(arrayp e3)

(vectorp e3)

(array-rank e3)

(array-dimensions e3)

(array-dimension e3 0)

(array-dimension e3 1)

(array-in-bounds-p e3 1 3)

(array-in-bounds-p e3 3 9)

Write a function which prints all the values of a two-dimensional array in a table. The function should work for any size two-dimensional array.

Enter the following.

> (setq v1 (make-array 6 :initial-element 'x))

> (aref v1 0)

> (aref v1 2)

232   ARRAYS

> (dotimes (i 6)
       (princ (format nil "~a ~a~%" i (aref v1 i)))
)

> (setf (aref v1 0) '(x y z))

> (aref v1 0)

> (setf (aref v1 1) 11)

> (aref v1 1)

> (setq v2 (make-array 4 :initial-contents '(a b c d)))

> (dotimes (i (array-dimension v2 0))
       (princ (format nil "~a ~a~%" i (aref v2 i)))
)

> (setf (aref v2 0) 0)

> (aref v2 0)

> (setq m1
       (make-array '(5 8) :initial-element "Hello ")
)

> (dotimes (i 5))
       (dotimes (j 8))
           (princ
               (format nil "~a ~a ~a~%" i j (aref m1 i j))
)
)
)

> (setq m2
       (make-array '(2 3) :initial-contents
                          '((a b c) (x y z))
)
)

> (dotimes (i 2))
       (dotimes (j 3))
           (princ
               (format nil "~a ~a ~a~%" i j (aref m2 i j))
)
)
)

Suppose the following expressions are evaluated.

LESSON 20

```
(setq e4 (make-array '(4 6) :initial-element 99))

(setq e5
  (make-array '(2 4) :initial-contents
                     '((a b c d) (2 4 6 8))
  )
)
```

What are the values of the following?

(aref e4 2 4)

(aref e4 0 0)

(aref e5 0 0)

(aref e5 1 0)

(aref e5 0 1)

(aref e5 1 1)

(aref e5 0 2)

(aref e5 1 3)

Does initializing an array (using either **:initial-contents** or **:initial-value**) limit the types of values that may be stored in the array?

Enter the following.

> (setf v (vector 1 2 3 4 5 6))

> (arrayp v)

> (vectorp v)

> (dimensions v)

> (dimension v 0)

> (aref v 0)

> (aref v 3)

> (setf (aref v 2) 22)

> (aref v 2)

Suppose the following expression is evaluated.

(setf e6 (vector 'a 'b 'c 'd 'e 'f 'g))

What are the values of the following?

(dimensions e6)

(dimension e6 0)

(aref e6 0)

(aref e6 1)

(aref e6 5)

Is a vector an array? If so, what is its special characteristic?

SUMMARY

Arrays in Lisp are defined using **make-array** (or **vector**). An array may be initialize using **:initial-element** or **:initial-contents**. A vector is a one dimensional array. Components of an array are accessed using **aref**. Predicates for these are **arrayp** and **vectorp**.

Information about an array is obtained using the functions **array-rank**, **array-dimensions**, **array-dimension**, **array-total-size**, and **array-in-bounds-p**.

Array-rank-limit, array-dimension-limit, and **array-total-size-limit** document system limitations upon arrays.

LESSON 21
Structures

Enter the following.

> (defstruct person
    name
    gender   ; male /female
    age   ; in years
)

> (setf george (make-person))

> (person-name george)

> (describe 'george)

> (setf (person-name george) "George Porge")

> (person-name george)

> (describe 'george)

> (setf (person-gender george) 'male)

> (setf (person-age george) 22)

> (describe george)

> (setf (person-age george) (+ 1 (person-age george)))

> (setf sue (make-person))

> (describe 'sue)

> (setf (person-name sue) "Susan Muzan")

> (person-name sue)

> (setf (person-age sue) 21)

> (setf (person-gender sue) 'female)

> (describe 'sue)

> (setf henry (make-person :age 34))

> (person-age henry)

> (describe 'henry)

> (eql (person-age george) (person-age henry))

> (setf ann (make-person :name "Anne Cann"
                        :gender 'female
                        :age 29
)
)

> (person-age ann)

> (person-name ann)

> (describe 'ann)

Suppose the following expressions have been evaluated.

(defstruct book
  author
  pages
)

(setf 'moby-dick (make-book))

(setf (book-author moby-dick) 'melville)

(setf 'tom-sawyer (make-book :author 'twain :pages 423))

What are the values of the following?

(book-author moby-dick)

(book-author tom-sawyer)

(book-pages tom-sawyer)

Assuming the preceding, write an expression which makes the structure for **moby-dick** have a length of 568 pages.

Assume the **defstruct** expression which defines a person structure (as at the beginning of this lesson) has been evaluated. Write a function which has one argument, a person structure, and which has the effect of increasing the age of the person by **1**. For example, if the function is named **add-a-year** and the value of **(person-age george)** is **23** then after **(add-a-year george)** is evaluated the value of **(person-age george)** would be **24**.

Enter the following.

> (defstruct person
      name
      (gender 'unknown)
      (age 0)
)

> (setf sam (make-person))

> (person-gender sam)

> (person-age sam)

> (describe 'sam)

> (setf (person-name sam) "Sam Kam")

> (person-name sam)

> (setf (person-gender sam) 'male)

> (person-gender sam)

> (setf (person-age sam) 34)

> (describe 'sam)

> (setf meg
        (make-person :name "Margeret" :gender 'female)
)

> (person-name meg)

> (person-gender meg)

> (person-age meg)

> (describe 'meg)

> (setf mary (copy-person meg))

> (person-age mary)

> (describe 'mary)

> (eql meg mary)

> (equal meg mary)

> (eql (person-gender meg) (person-gender mary))

> (equal (person-gender meg) (person-gender mary))

> (setf (person-name mary) "Mary Mee")

> (describe 'mary)

> (describe 'meg)

> (setf peg meg)

> (describe peg)

> (eql meg peg)

> (equal meg peg)

Suppose the following expressions are evaluated.

(defstruct book
  (author 'unknown)
  (pages 0)
)

(setf scarlet-letter (make-book))

(setf moby-dick (make-book))

(setf (book-author moby-dick) 'melville)

(setf tom-sawyer
  (make-book :author 'twain :pages 423)
)

(setf huck-finn (copy-book tom-sawyer))

What are the values of the following?

(book-author scarlet-letter)

(book-author moby-dick)

(book-author tom-sawyer)

(book-author huck-finn)

(book-pages scarlet-letter)

(book-pages moby-dick)

(book-pages tom-sawyer)

(book-pages huck-finn)

Enter the following.

```
> (defstruct person
        name
        (gender 'unknown)
        (age 0)
  )

> (setf pam
       (make-person :name "Pam Ana" :gender 'female)
  )

> (describe 'pam)

> (defstruct (student (:include person))
        major
        (year 'frosh)                    ; frosh, soph, jr, sr
    )

> (setf joe (make-student))

> (student-gender joe)

> (person-gender joe)

> (setf (student-gender joe) 'male)

> (student-gender joe)

> (person-gender joe)

> (student-year joe)

> (setf (student-name joe) "Joe Cool")

> (describe 'joe)

> (setf mark
       (make-student :name "Mark Kup" :gender 'male
                     :major 'Comp-Sci
       )
  )

> (person-name mark)

> (student-name mark)

> (person-gender mark)

> (student-major mark)

> (student-year mark)
```

LESSON 21

> (describe 'mark)
> (setf (student-year mark) 'soph)
> (setf (student-age mark) 19)
> (describe 'mark)
> (setf mack (copy-student mark))
> (describe 'mack)
> (setf mike (copy-person mark))
> (describe 'mike)

Suppose the following expressions are evaluated.

(defstruct book
  (author 'unknown)
  (pages 0)
)

(defstruct (biography (:include book))
  (subject 'unknown)
  birthyear
)

(setf roosevelt-in-retrospect (make-biography))

(setf inventing-america
  (make-biography :author 'wills
             :subject 'jefferson
)
)

(setf (biography-birthyear inventing-america)
  1743
)

(setf benjamin-franklin
  (make-biography :author 'clark
             :subject 'franklin
)
)

```
(setf (biography-birthyear benjamin-franklin)
  1706
)
```

What are the values of the following?

(book-author roosevelt-in-retrospect)

(biography-author inventing-america)

(biography-author benjamin-franklin)

(biography-pages roosevelt-in-retrospect)

(biography-subject inventing-america)

(biography-subject benjamin-franklin)

(biography-birthyear inventing-america)

(biography-birthyear benjamin-franklin)

What is the purpose of :include in defstruct?

SUMMARY

A structure is defined using **defstruct**. A structure definition specifies the names for its components.

Instances of the structure are then constructed by using **make-** with the structure's name.

A component of a structure is accessed by using the structure's name, a hyphen and the component's name.

Default values can be supplied with component names with **defstruct**. Initial values can be specified when **make-** creates an instance of a structure. **Defstruct** can utilize previously defined structures with **:include**.